Keith Floyd, veteran of many a heroic binge, has written the essential companion to that virtually pandemic ailment, the hangover.

From the creative to the delayed, from the mildly euphoric to the knock-out, Floyd investigates not just the physical symptoms of hangovers but also their psychological, emotional and spiritual manifestations. His counter-measures range from soothing recipes such as his interpretation of the famous Jeeves 'tissue restorer' entitled 'the Silly Sod' to heavy-duty cures for emergency use only.

Floyd also advances his own unique five-day detoxification programme, which consists of a deliciously light, cleansing diet plus a little gentle exercise. Throughout he combines humorous anecdotes with sensible, practical advice, which draw on a lifetime's experience of hangovers; and he also includes many sobering tips from his knowledgeable doctor friend, Hector.

If you have ever groaned in agony after excessive indulgence and awoken with that wicked, evil, throbbing I-wish-to-die feeling, *Floyd on Hangovers* is the book for you.

'Perfect for Floyd fans and anyone likely to suffer a hangover over the festive season'– Sunday Times

ABOUT THE AUTHORS

Keith Floyd was born in 1943 and educated at Wellington School, Somerset. Since then he has devoted his life to cooking, except for a few brief excursions into the army and the antiques and wine trades. Happily released from the rigours of running a restaurant by a chance meeting with David Pritchard, a BBC producer, he has now presented seven successful cookery series and written several bestselling books, of which Penguin also publishes *Floyd on Oz* and *Floyd on Spain*. When he is not hurtling around the world he spends his time in Devon, where he owns a pub.

David Pritchard grew up near Southampton, where he learnt to fish and lean expertly on five-bar gates while gazing out over the water meadows. He joined the BBC in Newcastle-upon-Tyne, where he first discovered the many variations of the dreaded hangover. He met Keith in his restaurant in Bristol and has since produced all Keith's TV series, for which they have travelled the world, filming as they go, inventing delicious cocktails, making new chums and staying up until quite late, really.

FLOYD ON HANGOVERS

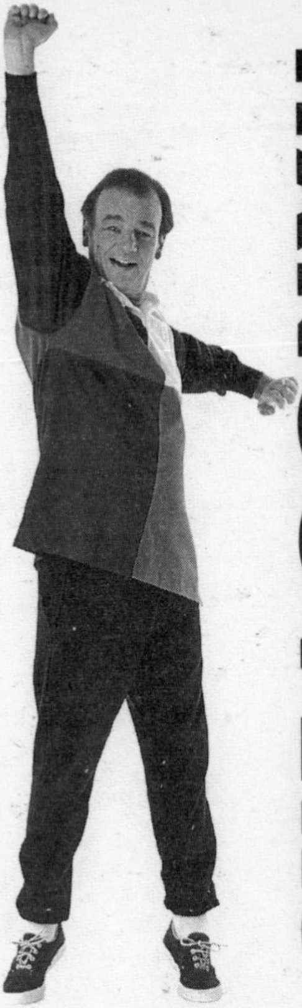

FLOYD ON HANGOVERS

HANGOVERS

**AN AUTHORITATIVE GUIDE
AND FIVE-DAY DETOXIFICATION
PROGRAMME**

**THE COMBINED EXPERIENCES OF
KEITH FLOYD AND
DAVID PRITCHARD**

SIGNET

PENGUIN BOOKS

Published by the Penguin Group
Penguin Books Ltd, 27 Wrights Lane, London W8 5TZ, England
Penguin Books USA Inc., 375 Hudson Street, New York, New York 10014, USA
Penguin Books Australia Ltd, Ringwood, Victoria, Australia
Penguin Books Canada Ltd, 10 Alcorn Avenue, Toronto, Ontario, Canada M4V 3B2
Penguin Books (NZ) Ltd, 182–190 Wairau Road, Auckland 10, New Zealand

Penguin Books Ltd, Registered Offices: Harmondsworth, Middlesex, England

First published by Michael Joseph 1992
Published in Penguin Books 1993
1 3 5 7 9 10 8 6 4 2

Printed in England by Clays Ltd, St Ives plc

CONTENTS

HANGOVER

The unpleasant symptoms that follow the drinking of too much alcohol. These include nausea, vomiting, intense headache, stomach pain and photophobia (sensitivity to light). The symptoms are caused by dehydration, irritation of the stomach lining and a degree of poisoning by the breakdown products of alcohol.

ACKNOWLEDGEMENTS

To all the bar staff, cooks, restaurateurs, late night drinkers, fishermen and philosophers all over the world, whose unselfish devotion to finding the elusive hangover cure has enriched our researches. Our thanks also go to Pam and Peter Stockley and all their wonderful friends in Melbourne, Dr Jan Perks, Dr Chris Gadd and the Hall family of Bristol.

INTRODUCTION

Many years ago *Private Eye* had a cartoon that amused me so much it has been indelibly etched on my mind ever since. It showed two dishevelled drunks at a bar, clearly several sheets to the wind, one saying, 'Actually, I used to be a £30,000 a year advertising executive until I discovered . . .' (At the time there was a series of vodka advertisements which implied that if you drank this stuff everything about your life, your hopes and your aspirations would improve.)

In a similar but unrelated way I was a perfectly contented, ordinary, moderately successful small town restaurateur, happily cooking *coq au vin* and brains in black butter for a small but select clientele; I had no cares, no worries, no great expectations, just a steady provincial life – until I met David Pritchard.

Late-night arguments, chaotic schedules, insecurity, international sake drinking competitions, the world of television – the mad, mad world of television – and thumping hangovers were something I knew little about.

Now after seven years of hurtling around the world with my chum Pritchard, I am used to waking up in San Francisco, Bangkok or Sydney feeling sick and tired of waking up sick and tired. We have dedicated our livers to our art and if from time to time we didn't take some sensible steps to counterbalance our absurd, satisfying lifestyle, we would be in a home for the bewildered.

So together, David and I, drawing on vast researches and experience, have thrown together a few ideas to help you keep fit and trim, bright-eyed and bushy-tailed.

Keith Floyd

David Pritchard.

HANG

ANATOMY
OF A HANGOVER

I have been sitting here now for at least an hour with a packet of frozen peas on my head — purely as an experiment, you understand. Out of my study window I can see the ducks busily sticking their bills into the thick mud of the riverbank, snaffling up the little juicy worms and *Crustacea*.

Inside my warm study, I make yet another attempt to put pen to paper to help explain the mysteries and miseries of the simple hangover. The paper remains stubbornly white except for the odd splash of defrosted ice dripping from my two-pound bag of *petits pois* which, at the moment, is acting as a turbo-intercooler for my tired old head.

Yesterday, I thought, erroneously as it turned out, that the best way to write about a hangover was to jolly well go out and get one. So in an altruistic moment I forced myself, over a long evening, to sample a range of drinks not generally known for their life-giving properties. As a piece of market research the exercise proved entirely worthless because after my second Flaming Lamborghini — a curious cocktail of Grand Marnier, chartreuse, Curaçao and Galliano — I was enjoying myself far too much to record how I was feeling. I do know, however, that I consumed several glasses of strong Algerian wine before the evening ended because my tongue had turned a bright shade of purple.

Recognising the Symptoms Fig. 9

Now, six hours later, staring at
this watery scene, I am reminded of John Betjeman's
aptly chosen words from 'The Arrest of Oscar Wilde
at the Cadogan Hotel':

> *He sipped at a weak hock and seltzer*
> *As he gazed at the London skies*
> *Through the Nottingham lace of the curtains*
> *Or was it his bees-winged eyes?*

The ducks, bored with their muddy breakfast, have
started to chase each other through the kingcups and
I, influenced by Sir John's poetry, sip at a weak hock
and Seltzer to revive my spirits and search every pore
of my being for inspiration. The *petits pois* have lost
their chill ages ago and are now a soggy plastic island
in my hearth, and Oscar's preferred morning reviver
is beginning to work its magic.

There are, I've decided, three main types of hangover.

THE DOUBLE WHAMMY

First of all there is the Double Whammy. This is a particularly wicked, heavy, throbbing, nauseating, sweatmaking, trembling type of hangover. It plumbs the depths of despair and it saps your strength and self-esteem. The physical and mental discomfort is so acute that many feel they have a permanent affliction and seek urgent medical help.

In order of seriousness this is as low as it goes, summed up to perfection by Kingsley Amis in the classic *Lucky Jim*.

Dixon was alive again. Consciousness was upon him before he could get out of the way; not for him the slow, gracious wandering from the halls of sleep, but a summary, forcible ejection. He lay sprawled, too wicked to move, spewed up like a broken spider-crab on the tarry shingle of the morning. The light did him harm, but not as much as looking at things did; he resolved, having done it once, never to move his eyeballs again. A dusty thudding in his head made the scene before him beat like a pulse. His mouth had been used as a latrine by some small creature of the night and then as its mausoleum. During the night, too, he'd somehow been on a cross-country run and then been expertly beaten up by secret police. He felt bad.

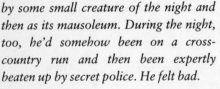

For a hangover of this magnitude the best cure, in my humble opinion, is a heavyweight reviver. Something that acts quickly, dulling the pain, placating the stomach and with enough vitamin C to put you on the road to recovery – I suggest a Bullshot.

Those in the know say this drink came from those heady days of the transatlantic cruise liners where good food, lively company and masses of drink were on hand twenty-four hours of the day. The barmen were highly experienced and acted more like psychiatrists and philosophers to their cosmopolitan customers. They were also wonderful alchemists, blending 'cures' from America and Britain to find the super cure – the big hitter.

I have decided to award a symbol of ferocity to each type of hangover and its relevant cure. For instance, to the Double Whammy and its cure the Bullshot, I shall award a triangle.

Your monstrous headache may in part be caused by the sudden change in concentration of alcohol bathing the brain and a morning-after drink containing alcohol, like this one, can add just enough alcohol to make the change more gradual. Do not, though, come to rely on this method of curing your hangover. You don't want to be on the way to your next already.

The Bullshot

Couple of generous handfuls of crushed ice
1 wineglass tinned beef consommé
Juice of 1 lemon
splash of Worcestershire sauce
1 teaspoon hot horseradish sauce
1 shot of vodka
Dash of Tabasco sauce
Yolk of 1 fresh, free-range egg
Salt and freshly ground black pepper

Pop the ice in a jug. Add the consommé, lemon juice, Worcestershire and horseradish sauces, vodka and Tabasco and stir until smooth. Pour into your favourite glass, until it is just over half full. Pop in the nice orangey yolk of the free-range egg. I stress this because it is important to use only the best-quality and freshest eggs from producers whose hens have been Salmonella-tested.

Add salt and pepper to taste. Do not stir. Swallow the contents of the glass in one gulp. The effect is quite bracing, but not for the squeamish.

THE TIME BOMB

This is an extremely naughty and deceitful hangover. It is when you wake up feeling quite wonderful. Oh yes, you say to yourself as you brush your teeth, how surprising, after all those tequilas and oranges and strong Czechoslovakian lagers, I haven't the slightest inkling of a hangover. Gosh, I must be in really good shape.

Then a couple of hours later, possibly in the middle of an important business meeting, the pulse starts to play ragtime, the healthy glow fades to a sweaty, greasy grey, the dive bombers of anxiety begin to attack. The room becomes smaller and you feel a desperate need to visit the bathroom. It is only a matter of time before you lose concentration and feel the full gaze of the assembled company focused on your feeble efforts to cover up.

This situation is quite frightening and can often lead to panic. One poor soul I know fled a BBC production meeting because he thought he was having a heart attack. He asked a colleague to drive him

immediately to the casualty department of the nearest hospital. Halfway there, with the car windows open, he started to feel better. His pulse had settled down and the fresh air was clearly doing him good. So he told his chum to stop overtaking streams of cars on the wrong side of the road and take him back to the office. As they entered the main reception area Scott Joplin started on his pulse again, the lift became unbearably hot and the feeling of panic returned. He asked his friend to take him home, where he felt sure he would die.

The secret here, I have found, is to know yourself. If you know perfectly well you've had a great deal to drink the night before but you are feeling no after-effects, then realise it is probably because you are still in a state of euphoria caused by the alcohol. This is the stage before which Mr Nice-and-Jolly changes the night shift with Mr Mean-and-Vicious. The only trouble here is that Mr Mean-and-Vicious has been caught up in traffic. I shall give this hangover and remedy a square.

Only TIME will reduce the level of alcohol in the body and nothing – not even black coffee – can speed the rate at which alcohol is removed from the bloodstream. But a remedy for this state, which will make you feel better, is a small dose of vitamins from the B group (you can buy these in tablet form from health food shops). Squeeze the juice from 3 fresh oranges and swallow a paracetamol (aspirin will irritate an already irritated stomach). Drink as much water as you can.

The vitamin B will help mend your frayed nerves. The vitamin C in the orange juice is generally good for you. The water will help rehydration and feed those cells starved of fluids. The mild analgesic will simply help the pain.

There is, I understand, a tribe in Polynesia who drink not because they like the feeling of well-being and confidence that alcohol sometimes gives, but because they consider the trance-like phase of an advanced hangover is the purest and most sacred state of mind they can achieve.

Apparently, they feel an inner quietness – a total oneness with nature and the elements – and sit for hours without moving, totally 'in tune' with the Creator. I sometimes travel up to London like this on the 7.15 from Bristol Temple Meads and before I know anything I'm at Reading.

I really am a believer in the Creative Hangover and over the years I have grown to give it the respect and recognition it deserves. Without the odd drop of wine some of the finest poems, symphonies and plays that celebrate the human spirit and grace the English language might never have been written.

After a few beers and a couple of glasses of good wine I can wake up feeling ... well ... jolly creative. There is no nasty feeling of nausea; no throbbing head; no acute feeling of remorse or paranoia. Instead there is just a slightly fuzzy, curiously distanced feeling. It is as if I'm being used as a homing device for all the muses floating around the artistic airwaves.

> My pen, which usually waits at the bus stop of inspiration for hours, practically wears itself out as words queue up to be used.

Curiously enough, writers like Scott Fitzgerald and Ernest Hemingway, men who liked the odd glass or three before retiring, used to be on fine creative form the following morning. Hemingway liked to leap out of bed and write standing up in his pyjamas, staring out over the hazy blue waters of the Gulf of Mexico. His eyes and his mind would be focused on the seabirds that screeched and circled above some wiry old man, fighting to keep his balance in a little boat as he played the big fish.

For the Creative Hangover may I suggest a reviver called the Sydney Sunrise? I award a circle.

The drink is an extremely gentle one and will provide sustenance as you go about your good works on this happy morning.

Sydney Sunrise

Into a blender squeeze the juice from 1 lime and add a dessertspoonful runny honey. Add the yolk of a free-range egg and top up with fresh orange juice. Whirr away for a few seconds, then pour into a glass over crushed ice and sprinkle with freshly grated nutmeg. It is quite refreshing and is such a happy drink.

Incidentally, as I make this wonderful drink I find it helps to sing the hymn:

New every morning is the love
Our wakening and uprising prove;
Through sleep and darkness safely brought,
Restored to life, and power, and thought.

How true.

HANG
CURES
FROM AROUND
THE WORLD

T he Norwegians say they have 'carpenters in their head'; while the French call it a *gueule de bois*, which literally means 'a wooden face'; the Portuguese say that 'their tide has gone out'; the Germans call it *katzenjammers* – a wailing of cats. It was some bright spark in America, after the First World War, who coined the word 'hangover'.

Attitudes to this condition around the world vary. In the Politically Correct times we live in, the hangover is generally frowned upon. You can be excused a hangover for the following reasons: a wedding, christening, birth, promotion celebration or getting a divorce – anything else is out.

I remember, once upon a time, the hangover was taken as a badge of office for the world-weary philosopher who had spent the entire previous night quaffing vast quantities of rough red wine and smoking disgusting French cigarettes while discussing the spurious delights of Leonard Cohen and Walt Whitman. But now drinking is out of fashion. On the hat stands outside the boardrooms of the movers and shakers of life hang multi-coloured bicycle helmets like luminous tropical fruits. Inside it is triple Perriers all round.

Fortunately, in the bars of **France** there is a quiet understanding bordering on respect for the poor sufferer. The good *patron* can tell by the way a customer sits on the bar stool – the telltale sag of the shoulder, red coals instead of eyes and a slight tremor in the hand department.

There is sympathy, instilled by hundreds of years of coming to terms with man's ceaseless fascination with the grape. And with the sympathy, help is closely at hand.

This is a heavyweight cure from a little bar near my old home in Lisle sur la Sorgue in Provence – I shall award it a triangle.

In a glass jug pour in 1 shot each of Pernod and dry Vermouth, and add 1 egg white and the juice of 1 lemon.

Stir vigorously and serve over crushed ice. It is creamy and potent.

In **Germany**, if you are feeling unwell with the *katzenjammers*, then a plate of soused herring washed down with a small glass of Pils should set you up. However, if you are feeling really under the weather, then just call in to any family-run chemist shop. There, among the mahogany, marble and the coloured bottles, a smiling pharmacist will soon make you a frothing glass consisting of a mild analgesic, vitamins B6, B12 and C, and a chalky alkaline base. The formula will be a family secret that has proven its effectiveness a thousand times. It is not just the drink, it is the pride and the happiness – yes, happiness – that's registered on the face of the pharmacist as you quickly gulp the brew and replace the glass on the pink marble counter. In a few minutes the oily black vultures of anxiety, nausea and dizziness will flap their leathery wings and take flight.

Try doing that in your High Street chemist and see what you get!

In **Australia**, after a particularly heavy night's drinking, it is customary to have a couple of steak pies with Rosella tomato sauce, washed down with a can of ice-cold Coca-Cola.

In **Spain** I asked a barman what the best cure for the *resaca* was. He cockily filled a large glass with a mighty gin, chartreuse and some violet liqueur. He placed it in front of me and in his halting English said, 'You drink two of these and you get *resaca*!'

'I don't want to get a *resaca*, nobody wants the *resaca* – I want to know what mends the *resaca*!'

I saw the soft light of understanding dawn in his eyes – and, when he'd stopped laughing and tipped the large glass of lethal alcohol down the sink, he told me – *almejas* or little clams, preferably eaten raw first thing, or steamed with olive oil, lemon juice and garlic till they open.

In **Puerto Rico** they are reputed to rub the juice of various fruits into their armpits. The astringent properties of lemon and limes are supposed to revive their sagging spirits.

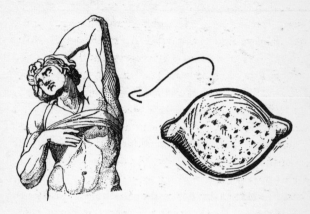

In **Sante Fe, New Mexico,** I tasted the finest margaritas ever. They were so good I must have had half a dozen, when suddenly my world started to spin and (with some difficulty) I had to retire early. The altitude (Santa Fe is around 6,000 feet above sea level) increases the effect of the alcohol and, I can verify, the severity of the hangover that follows.

A kindly barman at the San Francisco hotel administered unto me the following morning. He mixed a jolly friendly-looking drink, called a 'Geronimo', and I shall award it a square.

In a glass pop 1 generous spoonful of runny honey and 1 shot of tequila. Top up with full cream milk, stirring all the time. Add some crushed ice and a sprinkling of freshly grated nutmeg.

Fig. 3

In **Scandinavia,** where they are known to take the odd glass of strong drink now and then, they have for centuries trusted in the beneficial effects of saunas and massage to help tone the system. And in this new age of enlightenment – in which, I am happy to say, homeopathic and other alternative forms of medicine are becoming more popular – aromatherapy is particularly good for sorting out the evil hangover and bolstering the spirits. This is a wonderful, soothing cure given to me by my chum Trish Griffin of Wadebridge in Cornwall.

You mix the oils of lavender, peppermint and geranium with a base oil of sweet almond. Then you ask your partner to massage this fragrant balm into the nape of your neck for half an hour. The effect is blissful and, as a cure, it's more effective with a cold compress scented with geranium oil, on the forehead.

The only problem I can foresee here is that the people who believe in homeopathic cures are not really likely to get hangovers in the first place!

And now to **Ireland**. I feel my happiest and most fulfilled here among the white cottages, rainwashed streets and noisy bars. The hangover is not feared in these parts; in fact, it is hardly mentioned, a small pinprick of discomfort for an evening of spirited conversation, creamy stout, laughter, debate and sweet peaty whiskey.

A well-tried and trusted cure comes from a happy little bar called the 1601 in Kinsale. It is called a Battle Burger, named after the mighty sea engagement off Kinsale nearly four hundred years ago. It is really a thick, glutinous Irish Stew in a bun. As I write this I feel the description does not do it justice. The lamb and potatoes not only taste wonderful but provide nourishment and sustenance for an unhappy stomach.

Another Irish cure I can fully recommend and have put to the test a number of times is half-a-dozen oysters, followed by a pint of Murphy's. I asked my chum Hector, who is a doctor and knows about these things, why this should work.

'It's to do with the levels of zinc, old boy,' he said, somewhat mysteriously. 'Drink affects the zinc so if you drink you need zinc! Oysters contain this element in fairly large doses, which is one of the reasons they are regarded as an aphrodisiac.'

But that's another book!

HANG
NEVER
SURRENDER

When you wake up alone after consuming a whole dictionary of cocktails, your body is on red alert. This is what you must do after the eyes have been opened. Keep perfectly still. Imagine that you have a crate of unstable nitroglycerin lodged in your brain and that with one false move you'll be painted over the bedroom walls. It is important to take stock and to use the brain, however impaired, to assess the damage on the rest of the body.

Picture the brain as the busy centre of operations, bustling with uniformed personnel, large maps and ringing telephones.

'Brain to stomach, Brain to stomach, come in please?'

After a pause of a few seconds a faint crackle can be heard and then, 'Stomach here, Brain, badly hit [crackle, crackle], monstrous cocktails, you name it . . . [more static on the line] brandy, gin; we have too much acid on board . . . might have to bail out soon . . . over.'

'Brain to liver, come in, please? Over.'

'Liver here, Brain [obviously very angry]. What the hell's going on? My boys here handled the first few drinks without any problems, but, Brain, have you gone completely mad? You know we can only cope with 1/200th of an ounce of alcohol per minute;

OVERS

FROM CENTRE OF OPERATIONS. MESSAGE READS:
"WE SHALL NEVER SURRENDER!" STOP.

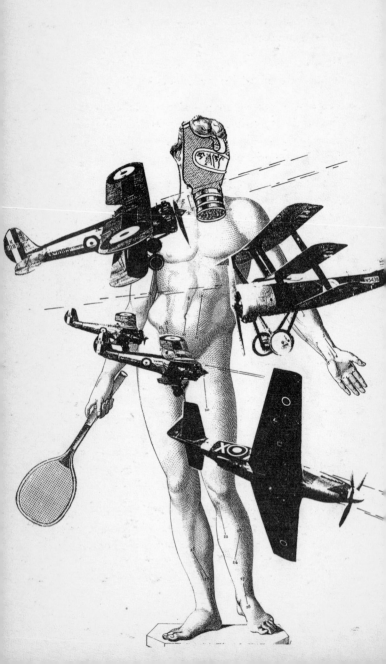

we've had to send the excess into the general blood supply, which means, of course, the heart has been pumping it, fresh, into every organ. Everything is affected and that means you, Brain.'

The Brain is a bit dumbfounded by all this and he makes one final call, to the kidneys.

'Everyone is complaining, kidneys, of dehydration. I hold you responsible for this, you've gone totally crazy and pissed away practically all the body's fluids. Everyone's parched; it's like a desert.'

After all this ringing around, the news isn't good. In the war room of the Brain, the grey cells examine the information collected. One of the grey cells, who looks a bit like James Mason, assesses the problem.

'Gentlemen, last night we were hit hard, bloody hard. The stomach was pulverised by waves and waves of high explosive cocktails. The liver put up a damned good fight but the buggers managed to parachute into the blood supply causing the kidneys to go berserk and lose masses of valuable fluids. As you know, gentlemen,' he says, pointing to the map of the body's nervous system with his long stick and twiddling his moustache, 'as you know,' he repeats, purely for dramatic effect, 'we have been partially overrun. All our major trunk roads have been hit and there is not one important installation in the whole of the territory that hasn't been touched. We need re-inforcements pretty damned quickly.'

The attractive young grey cell, with the nice tight uniform, sitting at the back of the war room, cranks her telephone and sends a signal for the body to go out and get help.

Now, this is your cue to get out of bed and make your way to the kitchen, to drink as much as you can of cold, clear water. This will help revive those poor cells starved of fluids and it will reduce the acid in the stomach.

A loud hurrah! goes up in the war room. The grey cells are hugging themselves with glee and, through soft focus, we see the pretty grey cell wipe away a tear of joy. James Mason pushes a few markers around on the map and says sternly, 'Gentlemen, the situation is still serious, we need to parachute urgent supplies of analgesics and vitamins into the system, to reduce the headache caused by dehydration and to neutralise those damned alcohol molecules that have hijacked the nervous system overnight.'

This is when you squeeze four or five oranges and drink the juice along with a couple of paracetamol tablets.

The whole war room by now is going mad. Above the scenes of joy you can clearly hear the sound of church bells clanging victory. A signal comes in, which a fresh-faced grey cell who looks a bit like the young Richard Attenborough, answers. 'It's the kidneys on the line, Sir; they say thanks for the water!'

Another signal comes in, this time the pretty grey cell with runny mascara picks it up. 'It's the liver, Sir; everything is returning to normal. Do you want to speak to him?'

'No,' says James Mason, 'just say we're sorry and we'll do our damnedest to make sure it never happens again!'

Fade up to the final strains of 'The Pomp and Circumstance March'.

THE END

HANG
WHY DO WE GET THEM?

I asked my chum Hector who, as you know, is a doctor, quite a successful one actually, until the drink got to him. He said it is all amazingly complicated but he would try to explain.

'Alcohol,' he said, as he dropped Angostura Bitters into a large gin and added a splash of water, 'depresses the normal workings of the brain. This makes us super confident (we think) and makes us feel we are having a terrific time!'

He takes a large draught and continues. 'Now, when the brain is working normally it supervises the flow of a very beneficial hormone called an anti-diuretic.' He looks over his glass to make sure I am paying attention.

'Now this anti-diuretic hormone really stops your body getting rid of useful fluids; if we didn't have it we'd be popping to the loo every five minutes or so.' As if to make a point he makes an excuse to visit the bathroom.

'However,' he continues on his return, looking much relieved, 'the more alcohol we consume the more of this vital hormone is reduced. Consequently, we spend a great deal of time ridding ourselves of more bodily fluids than we are drinking. Now the lack of fluid in the system causes dehydration, which can have a pretty nasty effect on the body's apparatus. This is why we get headaches and when dehy-

It's all right – it's just a temporary hormone imbalance!

dration is coupled with the effects of those nasty congeners found in drink, the dreadful by-products of the fermentation process, then the effect is worse. Oh, and alcohol also stimulates the production of insulin, which in turn reduces the blood sugar levels. This can cause drowsiness, faintness and hunger.'

He fixes me with a bloodshot eye (he has two but only one seems to have focused at the moment) to see if I fully understand.

'Why then,' I say, 'do we also feel nauseous and as if our stomachs are no longer parts of us?'

Hector looks anxiously at his watch; it has gone twelve and the pubs have been open for an hour. 'Well, as you know, the stomach produces acid to help digest anything that we put into it. Be it sweet little clams in a parsley and white wine sauce [I'm feeling a bit peckish by now], or a refreshing Thai chicken curry with lemon grass and fresh coriander. Whatever is put into the stomach inevitably meets the stomach acid in various quantities depending on what it is we have consumed.'

With that Hector tosses the last of his pink gin down his throat. He grabs his battered trilby and ushers me to the door, clearly bored with all this simple medical talk.

'But Hector,' I say, as the old Rover purrs through the country lanes en route no doubt to the nearest pub,

'why is it that one feels so sick after consuming a bit too much?'

'Well,' he says, narrowly missing a bewildered-looking pheasant, 'the alcohol upsets the body's metabolism and this causes a rise in acidity. Because all the cells in the body are dehydrated, the acid-base metabolism is altered. That is why we feel sick. That is why we feel out of sorts, depressed and full of anxiety. The brain is not able to do its proper job because the lines of communication have been tampered with. Only time, patience and the proper application of a few chosen elixirs can remedy the situation. In short, alcohol has the same effect on the body as a group of Hell's Angels turning up at the Bishop of Bath and Wells' garden party!'

The pub is in sight, Hector slows the car down. 'That'll be fifteen guineas, old boy,' he says as he moves his generous frame off the soft leather and strides towards the pub like a man possessed.

PS Hector is currently working on a hangover cure toothpaste. It will contain not only the usual ingredients necessary for clean teeth and healthy gums, but a mild painkiller and drops of vitamins C and B. The theory is that, as you brush, you will start to feel better with every stroke. By the time you finish your hangover is gone and your teeth are perfectly white.

However, as alcohol is known to reduce one's levels of concentration, Hector's toothpaste will not be ready until the end of the millennium. Meanwhile, it is absolutely marvellous for rubbing down paint.

Hector prides himself on his knowledge of anything alcoholic. As a doctor he has over the years assiduously consumed, for medical research purposes, strange fermentations from all over the world. In Mexico he nearly went blind after drinking vast quantities of 'home-made' tequila and in Hong Kong he was sick for days after quaffing 'snake wine'. He was told by his Chinese chums that this rice-based wine, in which half-a-dozen smallish snakes had been drowned, would be exceedingly good for his libido. Strangely enough, it wasn't.

But Hector is a game old dog and though he is vastly overweight you can always see him dancing at parties. In fact, he cannot tell the difference between the twist and the lambada, but it doesn't stop him dancing the night away. He argues that sweating off all the toxins from the alcohol through gentle exercise is extremely beneficial to his well being the following morning. This preventative activity would be a little easier for those round him to bear if only Hector had someone to dance with, developed a sense of rhythm and stopped spilling his drink.

Hector is a firm believer in the restorative powers of Fernet Branca, a nattily-bottled medicinal drink from Milan, which has been around for one hundred and fifty years. Like the German hangover cure, Underberg, it contains over forty selected herbs, has a high alcohol content and is good for promoting the flow of the gastric juices and giving a sense of well being. In fact, the Savoy Hotel make an extremely interesting reviver based on Fernet Branca.

The Corpse Reviver

1 measure of brandy
1 measure of Fernet Branca
1 measure of white crème de menthe

Put all the ingredients into a cocktail shaker with some ice. Shake and strain into a glass. Do not, under any circumstances, drive for the remainder of the morning.

If you have been foolish enough to drink three litres of Western Samoan Cabernet Sauvignon, before moving on to a slightly heavier port wine, significantly bottled in Hartlepool, then the three miserable-looking judges sitting at the end of your bed when you wake up will give you 9.8, 9.8, 9.9 respectively. If you really had wanted to beat this score, then you should have had several large Scottish ones before starting on the wine. However, this is a fine score, as the hamster gnawing away on your cortex will testify.

It is not just the alcohol but all those beastly congeners, so prevalent in the fermentation process in the making of red wine and port, that would have scored a direct hit on the intestinal tract and the nervous system. Very often chemicals are added to the drink to help make it look more attractive – brighter and clearer – and it is these chemicals,

which, combined with the amount of alcohol, are frequently the cause of the worst type of hangover. Generally speaking, brandy, dark rum, red wine, port and sherries are the worst offenders followed by Vermouth, beer, whisky and gin and then white wine, lagers and the purest of all – vodka.

With all this congener-laden alcohol on board the simple task of posting a cheque to pay the gas bill would become complex and so full of important decisions that just addressing the envelope, if you were able to find one, would seem like writing a summary of *War and Peace*. This is as low as it goes. You feel that you are on the wrong end of a telescope with 'The Big Eye' gazing down at you as you fumble around the bedroom trying to decide what's best.

This is the time when you need someone who is in a worse state than yourself. Talking about how bad you feel helps. If there is no one around, go to the nearest railway station and look at the guys who have been sleeping rough. Look at those faces ravaged by strong cider, Carlsberg Special Brew, metal polish and broken dreams. You may think you can hear the faint strains of a heavenly choir singing 'Never ever ever again'! You may also feel that it is only a matter of time before you join them. This is good. Do not dally too long. Stride strongly out through the bus exhausts and discarded Kentucky Fried Chicken packets of life. Cancel all appointments. Find a field, preferably with a small stream gurgling nearby, and ponder the marvels of nature. Soon an inner spiritual light will start to glow inside you and the hamster in your head will begin to snooze.

Now is the time to make a private deal with yourself that you must swear will be honoured for the rest of your drinking life. Never touch a drop of Western Samoan Cabernet Sauvignon again.

HANG
A HISTORY OF
THE HANGOVER

I f it were possible I would like to rub my magic food mixer and make a wish to go back in time to the kitchens of a chap called Hesiod of the Epicurians who lived in ancient Greece.

Now Hesiod loved entertaining and he would invite his chums around quite often to partake in a few glasses of vino and the odd banquet. In fact, Hesiod became so knowledgeable about food and drink that he wrote one of the first cookbooks in the world.

Anyway, Hesiod was a fastidious host and although he did not realise it at the time, his culinary skills and knowledge would influence the whole Mediterranean. Long after Greece became occupied by ravaging tribes from the north, Hesiod's cookery skills would live through his books encouraging the Romans to cook his way and later, much later, most of Europe.

One of Hesiod's regular visitors, apart from Socrates who usually became very moody and always left early, was Antiphanes. Like most people at Hesiod's parties if you weren't a mathematician then you were a philosopher and Antiphanes was a brilliant philosopher. He was known for his wit and

42

wisdom and would usually ignore the groaning tables of food that consisted of hundreds of oysters, stuffed geese, lobsters, roasted lamb and game birds, asparagus and fruit and concentrate on the heady, rich full wine. It was customary in those days to mix the wine with water and in fact few people among the chattering classes would have dreamt of drinking neat wine, except, of course, Antiphanes. He thought it much better fun to lurch from one group to another with a full goblet of ancient Greece's finest, discussing and arguing religion and astronomy, until the sun rose over the Aegean.

Some of the guests wore wreaths on their heads and around their necks; it was a fairly new thing and was designed to keep the alcoholic fumes at bay. The wreaths were woven from plants that were said to absorb and neutralise the vapours from the wine, and they were usually made from roses, violets and, most common of all, myrtle. They made a colourful crowd these Greeks, with their fine food, ornate goblets and colourful wreaths, while most of Europe was living on millet, gruel and porridge.

Antiphanes was usually the first to arrive and the last to leave. One morning as the sun began to warm the loveliest of earth's valleys, Nysa, where Bacchus the God of Wine, crowned with myrtle and laurel, would supposedly frolic with his nymphs, Antiphanes coined these immortal words, the first recorded hangover cure.

> *Take the hair, it is well written*
> *Of the dog by which you're bitten*
> *Work off one wine by his brother*
> *One labour with another.*

Antiphanes, 479 BC

HEIR OF THE DOG

My chum, a brilliant vet by the name of Nigel Taylor, from Plympton in Devon, discovered a hangover cure while healing a sick dog. He told me that in the late 1970s vets all over the world were taken by surprise by a new canine virus, Parvovirus, which killed dogs in their thousands.

Parvovirus caused severe gastro-enteritis, which resulted in the dogs' deaths due to shock and dehydration. But research into this new disease was to revolutionise completely contemporary ideas about dehydration and fluid replacement in animals. Nigel told me intravenous fluid therapy was helpful but not always easy to administer so new oral electrolyte solutions were developed to reverse the process of dehydration and electrolyte depletion, which leads to shock and death.

In Britain the most successful and widely used of these is Lectade. Lectade is a white powder that you add to water (one sachet to 600 ml/1 pint). It is used a great deal when dogs' lives are threatened by dehydration and post-operatively when rehydration is often essential.

Many vets worldwide have also discovered its useful potential as an excellent hangover cure.

The dehydration that usually accompanies hangovers responds well to rehydration therapy. Nigel assures me a pint of Lectade, with its not too unpleasant sweet taste, taken the morning after the night before, soon restores the average affected vet to something like physiological normality. It shouldn't happen to a vet, but when it does, oral electrolyte solutions are just the job.

Nigel always looks bright-eyed and bushy-tailed after a bender – also his nose is nice and cold. I wish he would get out of the infuriating habit of jumping on to my settee and chasing the next-door neighbour's cat when he comes to visit. Some degree of caution should be taken with this cure.

ET TU, FLOYD?

Everyone knows the Romans were even bigger on parties than the Greeks. A great deal of socialising and business were done chewing on the odd roasted dormouse, followed by forkfuls of stewed flamingo tongues and peacock's brains. In fact, if it walked, crawled, swam or flew then the Romans would cook and serve it at their parties. With most of Europe and North Africa under their domination the range of game, fruit, vegetables and wine was staggering and their parties went on for days.

Although Hollywood has portrayed the Roman feast as a free-for-all orgy with couples romping among the oysters and pomegranates, they were generally noble affairs where the drinking of wine was taken with much seriousness.

Pliny the Elder, a Roman official, wit and raconteur, was a great chum of the Emperor Vespasian and naturally was on the list for all the best parties. He didn't care much for drunkenness and, though he liked the odd glass himself, he regarded it as bad form to become totally blotto. Indeed, Pliny was a great observer of human nature and decided that he could benefit mankind by writing down a few well tried and trusted hangover cures of the day.

First of all he believed that prevention was better than cure and that the wearing of purple robes and the use of amethyst-studded drinking goblets would counter the fumes caused by the wine. Remember, the Romans were very superstitious people who believed strongly in the occult powers and before making any decisions would consult the oracle, a bit like Nancy Reagan today. Pliny also recorded that the wearing of parsley around the neck while asleep would alleviate the effect of the alcohol.

Pliny recommended, if on waking one is suffering, some lightly boiled owls' eggs for breakfast. However, if the hangover persists, he suggested one should partake of a dish of stewed eels.

I must add here a personal endorsement of the beneficial effects of eels. After a particularly mammoth evening's drinking in Poplar in London's East End a few years ago, I woke feeling decidedly rough. That morning I had to visit a Pie and Eel shop for some research into traditional British food. These shops are rare now but once upon a time they were on every street corner in the East End. With bleary eyes and a throbbing head I was handed a large steaming dish of stewed eels covered with a thick luminescent sauce made from parsley, incidentally a rich source of vitamin C. Expectant eyes looked my way for signs of gastronomic appreciation. I took a small mouthful, it was delicious. I took more this time, it was superb. In a few minutes my plate was clean. I was even given a round of applause and twenty minutes later I felt brilliant. Perhaps Pie and Eel shops were a legacy handed down from the Roman occupation?

Pliny, as you can see, was an extremely sensible chap; he wrote the first encyclopedia listing all the birds, plants and animals known to the Romans. He also took hangovers very seriously indeed and one of the most effective cures he found was garlic, mashed up with warm olive oil and drunk quickly. He believed that the garlic had a purifying effect on the blood and that the warm olive oil soothed the stomach. A well-known variation of this is common in France today and it is made by simmering salt cod in a little milk and oil; the recipe is on page 83.

A DRUNKARD'S TALE

Whoresheugh Castle stood on a steep cliff with commanding views over the surrounding countryside and the grey North Sea. The bitter north-east wind, flecked with sleet, whistled around the battlements, causing the sentries to shiver and pull their rough woollen shawls tighter round them as they waited, miserably, for dawn.

It was several hours since the music and laughter had died from deep inside the castle's walls. The main hall was, surprisingly, still warm and the smell of burnt fat and stale wine hung in the air. From the topmost portal, shafts of cold blue light as straight as swords cut through the hall's gloom, illuminating a score of sleeping bodies. Most of them were roughly sprawled around the long dead embers of the great fireplace, where the remnants of a roasted ox still hung from the heavy iron spit. A grey and grizzled wolfhound was busy stripping the tendons from a charred bone. The noise of the bone cracking in its powerful jaws woke Roger de Floyd, whose subconscious had been preoccupied chasing a stag on horseback over the Northumberland moors, flints sparking under the nag's hooves. With one swift movement Roger raised his heavy crossbow and aligned the metal bolt with the pulsating neck of the deer ... and then he woke up.

'In the name of the Lord, who beateth this drum in my head to cause my brain to make war with mine stomach?' he said, as he moved his heavy frame away from the long dining table. 'Did Beelzebub sup with us last night? All my kinsmen do here lie in death ... or is it slumber? Mine eyes feel hotter than the coals in Master Blacksmith's forge, 'twas a rough night.'

In the crepuscular light the bodies stirred among the debris from last night's supper. The bullrush matting covering the stone floor was wet and red with Bordeaux wine. Roger stirred some more and, filling his lungs with the fetid air, he bellowed for his page, Siward, to attend him. His roar was so loud even the sentry on the topmost battlement stopped relieving himself into the moat when he heard it.

'Hark! Our master has the voice of a thousand tormented demons and the day will be damned for all of us.'

'What is your gracious pleasure, my Lord?' said Siward, moving with caution through the moaning bodies.

'Canst thou not minister to me some sweet antidote to expel the perilous stuff that troubles the brain and weighs upon the stomach and purge it to a sound and pristine health?' muttered Roger, as he shielded his eyes from the cruel light.

Siward made his way down the stone stairs to the great kitchen. He knew exactly what his master needed. He had, after all, made it numerous times in the years since the old apothecary Bardolph had taught him when he first came to the castle.

...I understand thou doth spit feathers my Lord!

He busied himself adding senna to the cast iron pot of boiling water. This, he knew, purged the stomach of all its poisons. To this he added the pinky red stalks of ripened rhubarb, which quickly thickened the brew. He stirred the pot. Bardolph had told him that the rhubarb would help clean the blood and clear the eye. Then he added a jar of mead, a liquor made from honey, wine and wild herbs. This was fermented by the monks in their monastery on the nearby island of Lindisfarne. The honey would provide energy and the wine would restore good cheer and dull the aching head. He added two handfuls of lovage, which the Romans had used centuries before to ease the troubled stomach. Stirring gently, he put in the leaves of rocket, a common anaesthetic. Finally, just before straining, he immersed the stalks, leaves and seeds of wormwood into the stew. [Do not be tempted to make this at home, Children.] This was so potent that many of the entrances to the castle had a sprig of wormwood nailed to them to stop the evil spirits from entering. By the way, in later years wormwood was used to make absinthe – a favourite hallucinatory tipple of artists in France like Van Gogh, Manet and Toulouse Lautrec, but I digress.

He strained the pungent 'soup' into a great earthenware bowl and with extreme care made his way back to the great hall.

Some of the knights were being helped by their squires into their heavy chain-mail vests, in readiness for the long ride home. Their eyes followed Siward as he placed the steaming bowl in front of Sir Roger, who threw the dregs from his goblet over the wolfhound, which, blissfully undeterred, continued to gnaw away. Roger scooped up a full measure of the potion with his goblet and with some difficulty stood and raised the pewter vessel in honour of the assembled knights.

'Rid me of these spiteful and wrathful demons who have turned this banqueting hall into a charnel house, where despair and pain and the dull daggers of remorse now rule this merry kingdom. Bring back the ruby glow of rude health and rid me of this ache.' With that he emptied his goblet.

The sun, by now, was warming the sentries, who watched as the first party of knights straggled homewards, their steeds picking a delicate path through the heather as if aware of their masters' aching heads.

Roger emerged from his earthen closet, buckling

his heavy belt. The senna in the brew had worked quickly and life's fire had returned to his eyes. 'By God! I needed that,' he exclaimed. The knights who remained grabbed whatever chalices that lay among the pieces of stale bread and leftovers and made their way, as if for Holy Communion, towards the bowl.

During the Middle Ages vinegar and honey were widely used as cures. After the introduction of the spice trade, possets made from sweetened cream curdled with hot ale and eggs and flavoured with cinnamon, cloves, ginger and nutmeg were drunk. The thick mixture was sipped warm from pewter mugs and was extremely popular among the jolie young rascals of the day.

Occasionally, if I wake up with a slight head after too much wine, I will mix a wine posset, which not only works wonders but is also extremely delicious.

Wine Posset

For 2
1 tumbler milk
1 tumbler dry white wine
1 dessertspoon runny honey
1 teaspoon finely grated lemon zest
Pinch each of ground ginger, cloves and
   cinnamon and freshly grated nutmeg

Heat together the milk and wine in a pan until the milk has curdled and the brew is hot, then add the honey and lemon zest. Sprinkle with the spices. Strain through a fine sieve into two glasses and drink while still warm. It is simple, time-honoured and fortifying. For a naughtier version, substitute the wine for dark rum or whisky.

A YOUNG BUCK'S FIZZ

When the drinking of fortified wines became popular in the early nineteenth century a distant and long dead relative of mine opened a small coffee shop in the city of Bath. The upper classes came in their droves to take the waters at the Pump Room, to play cards, to have afternoon tea parties and a generally healthy time, a break from the noise and smells of London.

The young Regency bucks, however, needed more stimulation than the health-giving properties Bath Spa could offer. They spent their time eating rich food, gambling and being in their cups. Their revelries have become the theme for many a romantic novel but their late nights and their consumption of much Burgundy, Bordeaux, port and brandy provided my great-great-great-grandfather with a thriving business.

You see, many years before, Oliver Floyd had trained as an apothecary when he had learnt about alkalis and acids, the basic elements, the workings of the body and all that. He was a resourceful chap, reputedly a brilliant cook, but it was for his restorative cures that he became famous in this elegant city. The little brass bell above the door would herald the entry of the world-weary. Pale faces with dark-rimmed eyes and silk cravats askew would make for the tables furthest from the bright sunshine. Last night they had been cock pheasants, with shiny gold plumages, flashing under chandeliers, dancing the quadrille and drinking richly-flavoured punches. Now they seemed more like grubby town pigeons waiting expectantly for a few crumbs.

Oliver knew exactly what they needed – his now sadly forgotten pick-me-up. Oh yes, after just one glass, these pale ghosts would be transformed into hearty folk with strong pulses and soon the tiny shop would be shrouded in pipe smoke and would ring with the sound of laughter.

Oliver's cure was complicated. It consisted of: baking powder; an alkaline agent used to combat the acidity; a minute dose of strychnine (please do not be tempted to make this at home), which, in small quantities, is a stimulant; olive oil, which has a soothing effect on the stomach; and a large spoonful of honey for energy, but mainly to take the flavour of the oil away. He mixed all the ingredients together, added warm milk and one generous dash of lemon shrub, which was an alcoholic cordial made from lemons and rum. The foaming pale yellow mixture was usually drunk in one draught and 'Oliver's Cure', as it became known, was tasted by the gentry all over the West Country and beyond. Only one glass per day, per customer, was allowed following a nasty fright when a friend of Beau Brummel's had three in a row and collapsed with a mild dose of strychnine poisoning.

Oliver later changed the strychnine to caffeine and while he was at it altered his modest coffee shop to a chop house, where he would serve strong red fruity Burgundies, plus the best ports and champagnes that so many young people wanted to drink. After all, he decided, if one could make a good living curing 'the ache' then he rightly supposed he could make an even better one by giving it – and have more fun to boot.

WILL THAT BE ALL, SIR?

If I could pilot my gastronomic time capsule for meals future or dinners past then I might find myself riding into China with Marco Polo, cooking in the kitchens of the Medicis, tasting the first spices from the East with Vasco da Gama. Then I would plump for the not so far off times of the 1920s, to the days when the word hangover was first coined.

The life of Wodehouse's Bertie Wooster would have suited me well. The Medici kitchens would have probably been too hot and noisy, life on the road with Marco would have been terribly dangerous and I don't care either for long sea voyages or the prospect of sitting down to dinner night after night with Vasco over pickled pork and hard tack. No! If any life could suit, there would be none better than donning a brightly-striped blazer, crisp flannels and starting the day with a champagne cocktail.

The advantage of having someone of Jeeves' shimmering presence would be invaluable. Not so much for the pressing, dusting and opening-the-door duties that he would execute with the balletic grace and style of a Prussian officer, but more importantly for his unlimited knowledge of the gentlemanly art of reviving a frail, hungover Floyd.

I should call my own trusted valet Barrington and he would have had a rich and varied life, some of which had been spent working in the bars on New York's Broadway, before he entered the more dignified world of a gentleman's gentleman. I mention the bars of Broadway, not only because P. G. Wodehouse was fond of them but because they played an important role in creating many of the 'revivers' still used today. Large parties inevitably followed first nights in the theatre world and many an actor and producer would wait with throbbing head and nauseous stomach for the newspaper reviews to appear on the streets at dawn. This was when the barman's art came into its own. If the reviews were wonderful then champagne and plenty of it would have been the only reviver the thespians would have needed that morning. However, if they were unflattering, bordering on awful, then the spirits would have sagged, and the need for a physical and spiritual pick-me-up would have been paramount.

The following cure is probably the most famous morning-after reviver of all time.

The Prairie Oyster

1 measure of Cognac
1 tablespoon vinegar
1 tablespoon Worcestershire sauce
1 teaspoon tomato ketchup
1 teaspoon Angostura Bitters
Pinch of cayenne
The yolk of 1 free-range egg

Mix together all the ingredients, apart from the cayenne and egg yolk, in a whisky glass. Add a small pinch of cayenne and drop in the egg yolk. Drink down in one without breaking the yolk.

Barrington would have known all about these rather powerful American cures from his New York sojourn but, being a refined Englishman, he would have tempered his experience with the more delicate tastes of the English aristocracy. While I would be sleeping peacefully, with the gentle hum of the mid-morning traffic just audible through the Chinese silk curtains, Barrington would be busy in his pantry concocting this wonderful soothing remedy – for some strange reason known only to himself he called it Come the Revolution.

Come the Revolution

1 wineglass sherry
1 free-range egg
1 tablespoon caster sugar
Dash of double cream
Crushed ice
Small pinch of freshly grated nutmeg

Place all the ingredients, except for the nutmeg, in a cocktail shaker and shake vigorously. Strain into a whisky glass and sprinkle with the nutmeg.

The swish of the silk curtains and the glare of the midday sun would alert me to Barrington's silhouette holding a small silver tray and on it a crystal tumbler, the diffused lighting giving it a mystical quality, like the Grail itself.

An hour later would find me walking through St James's Park, scuffing the leaves and pondering what a jolly-luck-sort-of-cove I was to have such a gifted chap like Barrington to mix these elixirs. While all my chums would be hiding under the bedclothes promising never to drink again and assuring God that from now on they would only have the odd glass, if that, there would be Floyd, bursting with life's joys, worrying the ducks and looking forward to a late lunch of roasted rack of Welsh lamb, new season's runner beans and Jersey Royals, washed down with a bottle of Gevrey-Chambertin. Oh yes!

Barrington's pick-me-ups would soon become the envy of all my chums, especially when he made his famous Silly Sod!

The Silly Sod!

1 wineglass gin
½ wineglass bourbon
Juice of 2 freshly squeezed limes
Dash of Angostura Bitters
Lots of ginger ale
Mint and lovage, chopped

Mix the gin, bourbon, lime juice and Angostura over ice in a glass jug, then top up with ginger ale. Add some fresh mint and lovage. Stir and pour into a tall glass. Drink with lots of chums. It is guaranteed to put you into a good mood and make you feel as happy as you were before retiring.

However, I think I'll change my mind, if I may, about employing Barrington. Although he was jolly clever about mixing drinks and things and he could sew on buttons and be courteous to people when they visited, I would find myself becoming slightly riled by the fact that he always seemed to be enjoying a private joke. His 'revivers' continued to be particularly good throughout his term of employment, though they mysteriously persisted in having strange-sounding names. This one was a fine drink.

The Gormless Idiot

1 shot of Drambuie
½ wineglass double cream
1 dessertspoon runny honey
Finely grated zest of 1 lemon
Freshly grated nutmeg

Shake all the ingredients, except for the nutmeg, vigorously in a cocktail shaker and serve over crushed ice with a sprinkling of nutmeg.

Lastly, there was his Upperclass Twit.

The Upperclass Twit

1 shot of vodka
Juice from 1 small can of clams – eat the clams
*   later fried in a little olive oil and garlic and*
*   sprinkled with lemon juice*
Dash of Worcestershire sauce
Juice of 1 lemon

Mix everything together well and serve over ice.

A CAUTIONARY TALE

The effects of drinking too much of anything can be alarming. Beer or bitter in smallish quantities, say two to three pints a day, can be beneficial. I believe the ingredients, the malt and hops, help flush the system and have a purifying effect on the body. However, if you indulge, beware.

A friend of mine had a penchant for the odd glass of beer; in fact, his favourite tipple was Bass, a strong, hoppy brew made in Burton-on-Trent, the home of English bitter. Anyway, Bernard, on a visit to Bristol, consumed fourteen or so pints of this flavoursome drink. He spent the night snoring blissfully on my settee and the next morning a taxi called to take him to the station. Now, bitter in large quantities causes the stomach to go into overtime, creating large amounts of unwanted gas. As my front door closed, he let out a monstrous fart to greet the day. It was so loud, it made the next-door neighbour's spaniel bark. Bernard instantly knew he'd made a mistake, he also knew he needed another pair of trousers quickly. He rang my door bell without raising me. The taxi driver was becoming impatient, the train would be leaving soon; what to do?

He instructed the driver to go to the nearest Marks and Spencers, which fortunately was on the way to the station. While the meter kept running Bernard, with a strange ungainly gait, quickly selected a pair of trousers, forced himself to the front of a small queue of shoppers explaining that he had a train to catch and rushed as best he could to the waiting taxi.

He managed to board his train just as it was leaving. Clutching his green and gold carrier bag he made for the lavatory. As the catch slid home he breathed a sigh of relief. Bliss, sanctuary of sorts. As the train gathered speed, he threw the offending clothes out of the window. Relief. After he had cleaned himself he eagerly opened the carrier bag, looking forward to putting on a new pair of sensible navy blue corduroy trousers, a bit like the ones that were no doubt lying on the track among the fox-gloves and dandelions between Bristol and Bath.

Now, this is one of those moments that directors like Steven Spielberg love, when the camera tracks in very quickly, at the same time the camera operator is zooming out. The effect is magical, whatever concern registered on the face is magnified a dozen times by the distorting background.

Bernard opened the carrier to find a beige woman's cardigan. Nothing else but a beige woman's cardigan, size 8. In his haste he had picked up the wrong carrier bag and here he was locked in the loo hurtling through the English countryside at a hundred miles an hour, trouserless.

HECTOR'S TOP TEN TIPS

for the person
who finds it difficult to say no

1. It is absolutely vital to line your stomach. Food slows down the absorption of alcohol. The Irish know all about this and a favourite of theirs, before a mammoth drinking bout, is a plate of really creamy mashed potatoes mixed with a few chopped spring onions. However, my own preferred choice is tripe, nice white tripe, gently poached in milk and onions. Put on plenty of pepper and a dash of malt vinegar. This dish will please the stomach immensely. Hector says that protein, such as meat, slows down the absorption of alcohol more effectively than carbohydrates.

Incidentally, the Spanish and Italians take a small glass of virgin olive oil before a wedding or a christening party; it forms a protection for the stomach lining and will also slow down the rate at which alcohol is absorbed into the bloodstream, which is jolly good really.

2. If you smoke, and many heavy drinkers do, cut down, especially with a long evening ahead. Smoking makes you want to drink more. The medical reason is that alcohol is a vaso-dilator (that is, it causes the veins and arteries to expand) and nicotine is a vaso-contractor (this makes them narrower). As one Australian doctor said, 'Smoking and drinking together in any large amounts is like tickling your arse with a feather while hitting yourself on the head with a hammer' – the Australians are so graphic. So reduce your usual number of cigarettes by at least half and the evening will be much pleasanter, not to mention the morning after.

3. If you can, don't be scatty and drink lots of different drinks – stick to one. White wine is good because it contains fewer congeners; the darker and sweeter the drink, the more likely it is to cause a hangover. As the evening draws on, top up your white wine with a little still water. It will be enough to make you witty and engaging all night long and you will wake up next morning with a clear head and a fine untroubled conscience. Don't forget that fizzy alcohol, like champagne, is absorbed much more quickly into the bloodstream than the still variety.

You may also like to know that undiluted spirits are absorbed more slowly than diluted ones into the bloodstream. This is because the spirits activate the stomach lining, which produces a mucus to protect itself, and they also close a valve, the pyloric sphincter, between the stomach and the lower intestine, which helps slow down the passage of alcohol. This can give a false sense of security and delayed effect.

Dr. Hector's patent herring aid.

4. One very good way to avoid a hangover is to eat plenty of pickled herring. These oily fish are extremely good for helping the body to neutralise the effect of alcohol. If you manage to eat the odd fillet after each drink then you will wake up refreshed and relatively untouched by the ravages of strong drink.

Hector has a custom-built pocket in his dinner jacket where he can slip a specially adapted plastic container full of marinated herring fillets. During the evening, in between drinks, his hand will dart to the special pocket and he slips the odd herring fillet down his throat. You can drink vast quantities of alcohol using this method, but be prepared for a fairly solitary evening.

5. You must have lots of fluid before retiring to counter the diuretic effect of the alcohol. It still applies even if you've been following this invaluable advice and lining the stomach etc. It will not reduce the level of alcohol in the body, but it may make you feel better. So, whether you feel like it or not, and you won't, I promise you, be disciplined and drink at least a pint of water. Overnight your kidneys and your liver will be hugging themselves with glee and you will feel the difference in the morning.

6. On returning home, go immediately to the kitchen, quarter three oranges and arrange them neatly on a plate. Wrap them with clingfilm so they won't dry out. Then carefully put the plate at the side of the bed within arm's reach.

In approximately four hours' time you will wake up with a raging thirst. It is the sort of thirst that John Mills had in that classic British film, *Ice Cold in Alex*. A group of soldiers were stranded behind enemy lines; they had run out of petrol and had been forced to drink the water from the radiators of their stranded vehicles. A relentless sun beat down on them as they struggled through the shifting sands of the merciless desert – and the only thing that kept them going was the thought of making their way to a marble bar counter on which was a frosted, golden glass of Carlsberg lager with beads of condensation. They nearly went crazy at the prospect of putting their parched lips to the cold glass – but I digress.

At first you will forget about the oranges, then, after some uncomfortable decision-making about whether to get out of bed and fetch a glass of water, you'll remember them. This will make you so happy. Rip off the clingfilm and suck the sweet juice from the segments. Remember that the vitamin C is jolly good for you and the juice does wonders for the thirst. Do not use less than three oranges to slake your thirst. You will only feel like having more and have to get out of bed. In this situation more is better than less. (Hector has found after some heavy nights he has needed up to ten to do the trick!)

7. Have kippers for breakfast. Lovely golden grilled kippers — naturally smoked with oak chippings, of course. After grilling them for five minutes or so, it is important to serve them with the juice from a whole lemon. You see, your stomach will be feeling terribly acidy after quite a bit to drink and the introduction of yet more acid to an already queasy tummy might not seem the best of ideas. However, the opposite is true — the lemon juice will cause your stomach to speed up the production of alkalis — your very own nature cure for an upset tummy. We all know that oily fish is good for you. Anyway kippers are quite delicious and give you a healthy thirst to be slaked by pints of mineral water and fruit juice.

PS My researches have revealed that the first herring was smoked by an extremely clever gentleman in Seahouses, Northumberland, during the middle of the nineteenth century. For hundreds of years this windswept village had been a bastion for fearless herring trawlermen and crabbers with hearty thirsts. Local knowledge tells me that the recuperative power of the kipper has been well known in those parts for over a century.

8. Keep a jar of cockles in your pantry and on rising after a particularly rough night, unscrew the cap — you will hear a satisfying 'plop' as the seal is broken and instantly your nostrils will tingle with an infusion of vinegar and shellfish.

Before draining the vinegar, breathe deeply from the jar — the fumes will help to clear your head. (This, Hector must admit, doesn't work for everyone. His wife Naomi tried it, turned a sort of grey-green and was violently sick.)

Tip the cockles into a small bowl, sprinkle with white pepper and scoop up as many as you can with thumb and forefingers. Eat with gusto accompanied by processed white sliced bread and butter.

In twenty minutes you will be feeling quite wonderful. Do not move too far away from the bathroom during this period.

9. Eggs, or rather the yolks of eggs, are a particularly good source of protein that an alcohol-ravaged stomach finds quite soothing. This is a wonderful bracer first thing in the morning. In a tall glass put the nice orange yolks of a couple of free-range eggs. Then add the juice of 1 lime, a dessertspoonful of runny honey, and a small shot of Drambuie. Top the lot with fresh orange juice and stir like fury, adding ice.

Why should I do this? Well, first of all, the eggs, as Hector has already mentioned, are good for protein and food for the stomach to work on. The honey is great for energy. The lime and orange juices are a source of excellent vitamin C and the Drambuie soothes the aching brow and makes it more fun.

10. Kingsley Amis in his book *On Drink* suggested that there is no more pleasurable or effective cure than to make love, vigorously and passionately, to your consenting partner, the following morning. This is something that really does work and for some chemical and medical reason would be impossible the night before.

Shakespeare put it extremely well in conversation between Macduff and the humble witty porter in *Macbeth*.

MACDUFF *(after hanging one on the previous night): What three things does drink especially provoke?*
PORTER: *. . . lechery, Sir, it provokes and it unprovokes, it provokes the desire, but it takes away the performance; therefore, much drink may be said to be an equivocator with lechery. It makes him, and it mars him, it sets him on and it takes him off; it persuades him; makes him stand to and not stand to. In conclusion, equivocates him in a sleep and giving him the lie, leaves him.*

How true and how annoying.

HANGOVERS The causes

Dehydration Alcohol is a diuretic and causes you to pass, as urine, more liquid than you are taking in. So drink plenty of fluid (non-alcoholic!), which may make you feel better. It will not reduce the level of alcohol in the body. Only time can.

Low blood sugar Alcohol stimulates the production of insulin, which in turn reduces the blood sugar levels. This causes drowsiness, faintness, trembling and hunger.

Poison Impurities in alcoholic drinks can cause a type of poisoning. The acid in the drinks can also cause stomach upsets.

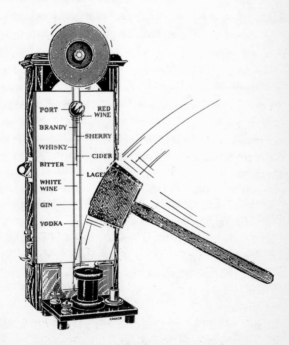

THE DARKER AND SWEETER THE DRINK the MORE LIKELY IT IS TO CAUSE A HANGOVER

HANG

THE FIVE-DAY DETOXIFICATION PROGRAMME

INTRODUCTION

I have been to the abyss and looked over and what did I see? Corpulence, high blood pressure, misery, tiredness and, in the far distance over this grim landscape, a cloud of dust kicked up by the hooves of the Pale Rider.

The ideal way to follow my programme is to take a few days off. However, if this is impossible then sensibly construct it round your work schedule. If you do have to attend business lunches in pubs and restaurants, order simply grilled chicken or fish with a fresh salad. Also, if you find the breakfast a little sparse, then top up during the morning with apples, pears, nuts (not too many of these, though, as they are high in fats), a freshly scrubbed carrot and a stick of celery; in fact, do this whenever you feel peckish. Concoct your own fruit cocktails in the blender using bananas, pineapples, peaches and citrus fruits, and add crushed ice and perhaps yoghurt. The range of tastes is endless.

Because I am a cook and not a chemist, I have designed this plan for people who love to eat and find sticking to diets difficult. What I have done is to

provide you with general guidance that will enable you to achieve your objective — to cleanse and rejuvenate your system.

Throughout the 1970s and 1980s, diets have been extremely fashionable, not to mention lucrative for scores of authors telling us it is wrong to eat this and it is right to eat that. Very often the diets have been contradictory. But there are seeds of common sense scattered liberally throughout any system you pick up from the bookshelf.

But the inspiration for my plan came from the Monastery of Osera in Galicia, Spain, which we visited during a filming trip. This was where Graham Greene coverted to Catholicism and it was where I first saw the sense in a simple and healthy diet using fish, chicken and vegetables as a base. I suppose the credit should really go to St Benedict, who in the sixth century first laid down that monks should be vegetarians. However, he conceded they should be allowed to eat fish and shellfish, but only the aged and infirm of the brethren could consume the red flesh from quadrupeds. It wasn't long before the monks cottoned on to the fact that St Benedict had not mentioned chickens. So they had them fried, roasted, boiled and grilled and always served them with large healthy portions of organically-grown vegetables from their immaculate monastery gardens. It is not a coincidence that the pale meat and delicate flavour of chicken has been traditionally linked with meekness and innocence, so much so that it was commonly eaten by all good Catholics as a compromise dish during Lent when meat was forbidden. Red meat, on the other hand, has long been associated with aggression.

As I waited in the coolness of the monastery dining room, while the film crew were getting ready, I watched the monks set about laying their long tables for supper. Several of the men were in their seventies but moved round the large medieval refectory like teenagers; their skin was flawless and their eyes shone with health and happiness. I looked at the film crew, who were busy shifting lights, and they seemed unhealthy, overweight and generally in poor condition compared to these men double their age (not you, Clive, it's the rest I'm talking about).

Like Sir Perceval searching for the holy grail, I saw an important clue looming before me – a sort of sacred light bulb went off in my head. So, when filming had finished and the crew were busy packing all the equipment away, I talked to the monks, through my trusted interpreter, Moncho, and gradually they told me about their diet and their lives. As the soft evening light shone through the ancient cloisters, the monks were amazed that anyone could possibly be interested in what they ate. They smiled deprecatingly as they described their midday meal of steamed fish on a bed of sliced peppers and potatoes; chickens sautéed in olive oil and garlic and tossed warm in a fresh salad; dishes of clams and mussels taken fresh from their unpolluted waters; lots of newly-baked warm bread eaten with quince jelly and a mild cow's milk cheese from their sheltered valleys; all washed down with the sharp white wine of the area, diluted with a little water.

> **Their menu was varied but it had a strong pattern of freshness and lightness.**

We chatted until the sky turned a bright violet and became studded with stars that stood out clearly in the frosty air. On the drive back to my hotel, I was determined to blend the monks' uncomplicated diet with various cleansing dishes and simple cooking methods I have picked up in my travels around the world.

Let's face it, after years of eating rich food, always a glass in hand, staying up late with new-found friends, there has to come a time to say stop! That's enough, thank you very much. It is time to give the liver a rest, the stomach a holiday and the whole metabolism a tonic.

THE ESSENTIALS OF MY FIVE-DAY PROGRAMME

The first thing to remember is that for the next five days there will be no highly seasoned foods (yes, Hector, your vindaloo goes out of the window); no tough, red meats; no rich, fatty and fried foods; no cakes or pastries, and hardly any alcohol either (just a couple of glasses of white wine on your fourth and fifth days as a reward for being so good).

I firmly believe that wine in sensible quantities can be positively beneficial and I cheer up enormously when I read reports that a generous intake of wine is quite the thing for lowering the levels of cholesterol and cleansing the arteries. Incidentally, I cheer up even more when I read that jogging and weightlifting are really bad for you. And I positively fall over with glee when I learn that teetotallers are in serious danger in later life from all sorts of diseases, nothing too serious you understand, because their systems have not been continually flushed with the health-giving properties of red wine and best bitter. But I digress . . .

If you start my diet plan the morning after a monstrous binge, and I suspect many of you might, then there are a few important points to remember. First of all, it is vital to drink plenty of water and fruit juice, around six to eight glasses each day. If you've read and understood the book so far, then you will know all this fluid will help the body cells damaged by dehydration. It will also assist the body in getting rid of waste products created when the metabolism breaks down fats.

Fruit sugars, or fructose, are brilliant for helping to repair the poor old damaged brain cells punished by a seemingly endless bombardment of booze. You can't go wrong by having a couple of bananas. In fact, sugars generally are good for the 'morning after', not just because they give you energy but, more importantly, they have a stabilising effect on the liver and top up the sugar glycogens sorely depleted by the liver's valiant battle with last night's intake of alcohol.

If you stick to my plan, your intake of protein – the basis of all life and the main constituent of body cells – will be normal. Remember, this is not a high protein diet but a light, fresh, nourishing one designed to cleanse and tone your system. Also, just in case you are worried, your daily supply of vitamins and minerals, essential to help regulate and control the normal functions of the body and to give you a sense of well being, will be amply catered for over the next five days. The rest is entirely up to you.

If you do stray off the path of righteousness once in a while, don't panic, just sensibly extend the plan to make up for your poor behaviour.

Also, remember it is vital to have plenty of fresh air and exercise. So, instead of taking the car for shortish trips, walk. Go with a chum to the baths and swim a few lengths. Exercise in whatever form helps sweat away those nasty toxins. You might well think that because you will not be drinking alcohol (except perhaps for the odd glass towards the end of the plan, and I do mean the odd glass of white wine – organically produced, if possible, because it contains fewer additives), you will have some difficulty in sleeping without its tranquillising effect. However, the very opposite is the case and a deeper, sounder and more restful sleep will be enjoyed as a result of your abstinence. If you follow this plan you will be fitter, fresher and sleep the peaceful sleep of an untroubled baby rabbit.

Bon appetit!

D A Y 1

BREAKFAST

Wear something light and cheering – do not get overheated and do not sit down. Cut a honeydew melon in half, scoop out the pips and devour the succulent green flesh with a spoon. Catherine de' Medici, who was renowned for going on the odd bender, used to swear by the restorative powers of melons. Your palate will feel instantly refreshed.

Take note. No coffee or tea will be allowed on this plan. They are diuretics; that is, they make you pass water and lose much needed body fluids. To accompany the melon, drink 600 ml (1 pint) water with the juice of 1 lemon squeezed into it. Then have a bowl of creamy plain yoghurt with some fresh fruit, like strawberries. The yoghurt will help soothe the tummy and the fruit, high in sugars, will please the old brain. If you are still hungry, then have a slice of wholemeal toast with Gentleman's relish. The carbohydrate in the toast will restore those depressed blood sugar levels.

Now it is time for exercise – a brisk walk to create a light sweat and help rid the body of those naughty toxins. Going for a walk will not lower the level of alcohol in the body, however. The alcohol will be mainly metabolised through the body at a fixed rate.

Put on your favourite anorak and fill the pockets with apples and pears. As you walk take in deep breaths, and remember the figure five.

Inhale for five steps
Hold for five steps
Exhale for five steps

Do this five times every five minutes. My editor, never having walked a step in her life, asked me why you should do this. Because it gets the circulation going and it clears the head, that's what I say.

If you are confronted by a large hill concentrate your mind on the area immediately in front of you and think of a tune that matches the speed of your walk. *Onward Christian Soldiers* is quite good. I use this frequently for hills, and it encourages me to whizz up them. 'Onward Christian Soldiers marching as to war . . .' etc., etc.

However, on the flat bits, as I stroll merrily along Devon's country lanes filled with primroses and cow parsley, I recite the 'Charge of the Light Brigade'. I am sure Lord Tennyson wrote this hearty poem after he'd 'hung one on' the night before, with brisk walking in mind. 'Half a league, half a league, half a league onward. All in the valley of death rode the six hundred . . .'

If possible, a brisk walk by the sea does wonders for the old head and respiratory system. Usually when I wander the rocky coast of Devon with the soft turf under my lightweight walking boots I recite out loud that fine poem, 'A Wet Sheet and a Flowing Sea' by Cunningham.

> A wet sheet and a flowing sea,
> A wind that follows fast
> And fills the white and rustling sail
> And bends the gallant mast;
> And bends the gallant mast, my boys,
> [I like that bit]
> While like the eagle free
> Away the good ship flies, and leaves
> Old England on the lee.

After an hour and a half spent walking you will feel revived and refreshed and soon, like the first snow-drops of spring, you will start to feel pangs of hunger – it is time for lunch.

LUNCH, DAY 1

Hampshire Chalk Stream Watercress Soup

Every time I have this refreshing and cleansing soup I think of my misspent youth fishing the River Itchen in Hampshire (mostly illegally). It is a beautiful river, gin clear and fringed with the most delicious plump and peppery watercress I have ever tasted.

I used to get up very early in the morning and cycle along a muddy path to a lonely stretch of water. There I would watch as my bait, usually a red worm,

"I thought I caught a fish alive!"

would be propelled by the currents and eddies, until it caught the attention of a fine brown trout or, better still, a salmon. There can be no more pleasurable thing on earth than to fish a swiftly flowing stream, listening to the shriek of the moorhen while munching on freshly picked watercress.

Serves 4

1–2 large bunches of watercress
1 large potato, peeled and diced
1 onion, chopped
1.2 litres (2 pints) chicken stock (home-made or use the liquid variety you can now buy in tubs)
Salt and freshly ground black pepper
Dash of lemon juice
4 tablespoons single cream

Wash the watercress and cut off the thick stalks. Keep back a few of the leaves to garnish. Cook the rest of the watercress, potato, onion and stock in a large pan for 20 minutes. Allow to cool slightly, then liquidise, in batches if necessary, in a food processor or blender. Return the soup to the rinsed-out pan and heat through. Season to taste with salt and pepper. Serve in large bowls with a dash of lemon, a tablespoon of cream and a sprinkling of watercress leaves.

1

Summer Vegetable Soup (*Soupe au Pistou*)

A wonderfully robust cure-all for the morning-after syndrome as the *Floyd on France* film crew will testify (with the exception of my trusty cameraman Clive, of course).

Serves 6

olive oil
2–3 cloves of garlic, chopped
350g (12oz) tomatoes, skinned, seeded and chopped
50g (2oz) dried white haricot beans, soaked overnight and drained
1.75 litres (3 pints) cold water
Few small new potatoes, halved if necessary, and scrubbed
225g (8oz) courgettes, chopped
Salt and freshly ground black pepper
225g (8oz) green beans, topped and tailed
225g (8oz) broad beans, or peas, shelled
Couple of handfuls of fine vermicelli
good handful of basil leaves
Parmesan or Gruyère cheese, finely grated

Heat 1 tablespoon of oil in a large pan and sauté 1 clove of garlic. Add the tomatoes, haricot beans and water, bring to the boil and simmer for about 20 minutes. Pop in the potatoes, courgettes and salt and pepper to taste and simmer, covered, for a further 25 minutes.

Now add the green beans, broad beans or peas and vermicelli and cook for a further 10 minutes, or until all are tender. Taste to check the seasoning.

Meanwhile, pound together the basil and remaining garlic with 3–4 tablespoons of olive oil in a pestle and mortar, or in a blender, until you have a smooth, thick paste. Stir in a tablespoon or so of the hot liquid from the soup. Serve the soup in bowls, spoon in the *pistou* and sprinkle in grated Parmesan or Gruyère cheese. In my opinion, you can't have too much basil in this soup and do make more of it if you wish.

Winter Vegetable Soup

I have been reading my *Boys' Own Bumper Book of Poetry* recently, searching for a rich and descriptive poem about soup – sadly, there is none. Most of these so-called poets, it strikes me, spend their time writing about unrequited love, the attractiveness of the countryside and things like that, and totally ignore the beauty of soup.

Do use really fresh, top-quality vegetables for this soup as there is no stock to help the flavour.

Serves 6

900g (2 lb) mixed vegetables, for example:
  onions, celery, swede, leeks, carrots and
  potatoes, peeled and roughly chopped
Salt and freshly ground black pepper
10 thin slices of white bread
150g (5 oz) Gruyère or Emmenthal cheese,
  grated

Pop all the vegetables into a large pan. Add enough boiling water to cover and season to taste with salt and pepper. Simmer the soup for 30 minutes, or until the vegetables are tender. Mash the vegetables with a fork, stir well and pour the soup into an ovenproof casserole. Float the bread slices on top, sprinkle with the cheese and brown in a preheated hot oven until golden and bubbly. Serve with crusty bread.

To drink, have one pint of pure water with the juice of 1 lemon, of course.

1

In the afternoon have as much fresh air and exercise as you can. If you are bored with walking get a bike, you can see so much more. Don't feel self-conscious about walking up the tiniest of hills even though your bike may have eighteen gears. Cycling, like ornamental pastry making, gets better with practice. By the third day you will notice the difference. Keep to the same circuit – say no more than six miles of quiet roads and, if you're lucky, gentle rolling countryside.

As I ride on my trusty Raleigh 'Ozark', I recite that joyous poem, 'A Laughing Song', by William Blake at the top of my voice.

When the green woods laugh with the voice of joy;
And the dimpling stream runs laughing by;
When the air does laugh with our merry wit,
And the green hill laughs with the noise of it.

It is difficult to feel depressed and unwell while doing this and don't be put off by the faces and stares of passers-by – they're envious, that's all.

Cream of Salt Cod (*Brandade de Morue*)

This is a classic cure in France for hangovers. You need a little foresight to soak the salt cod overnight – if you are that sensible then you probably won't get a hangover anyway. It is soothing and delicious, though quite rich. Your stomach, after this, will start behaving like labrador puppies running through spring meadows.

Serves 4

900 g (2 lb) salt cod, soaked overnight – change
the water several times if the fish is very salty
– and drained
450 ml (¾ pint) olive oil
450 ml (¾ pint) hot milk
Juice of 1 lemon
Freshly grated nutmeg
Freshly ground black pepper
Croûtons

Put the drained cod in a pan and cover with cold water. Bring to the boil and simmer for about 10 minutes. Lift out the fish and, when it is cool enough to handle, remove the skin and all the bones. Flake the flesh.

Put the fish in a heavy-based pan, and add a quarter of the oil. Over a low heat, mash the fish to a purée using a wooden spoon, slowly adding the remaining oil, until the mixture resembles dough. Gradually mix in the hot milk, until the fish has the consistency of creamy mashed potatoes. Take care not to over-heat or the mixture will separate. Stir in the lemon juice, add nutmeg and pepper to taste and serve with croûtons.

1

Fettuccine with Pesto Sauce

If your stomach was allowed to decide for itself what went into it, then surely pasta would be at the top of its list.

Serves 4

450 g (1 lb) thin pasta, like fettuccine or
  linguine
Salt
Parmesan cheese, finely grated

For the pesto sauce:

5 tablespoons virgin olive oil
2 cloves of garlic, quartered
4 tablespoons basil leaves
1 teaspoon salt
4 tablespoons flat-leaf parsley
1/4 teaspoon freshly grated nutmeg
1 oz (25 g) Parmesan cheese, finely grated

To make the sauce by hand, pound 2 tablespoons of the oil, the garlic and basil in a mortar and gradually beat in the remaining oil. Add the salt, parsley and nutmeg and pound until reduced to a paste. Finally, stir in the cheese.

If you are making it in a processor or blender, whizz all the ingredients, apart from the cheese, until well mixed. Stir in the cheese.

Boil the pasta in plenty of salted water until *al dente*. Drain, reserving a little of the cooking water, and serve on warmed plates, adding a little water to prevent it drying out. Serve accompanied by the pesto and the cheese.

To drink, why not try this fabulous fresh fruit cocktail.

To the blender add a handful of crushed ice. Then add a quarter of a honeydew melon chopped into chunks. Peel and stone a ripe peach and pop into the blender. If you can afford it and your supermarket has them, add the fruit of half a mango, which you have peeled and sliced.

Finally, add the juice from 3 oranges. Whirr away for a few seconds, until the machine has blended the fruit and the ice and serve in a tall glass – quite superb.

Now have a short walk, nothing strenuous, and retire early.

DAY 2

Make sure you are well stocked up with melons because, as you know by now, breakfast starts with half a melon and a pint of honest water with the juice of 1 lemon added. Follow it with yoghurt, fruit and toast.

You will be feeling a great deal better than you did on Day 1. So much so that you might be persuaded to say, 'That's it, I'm cured, I can't wait to have a pint at lunchtime with all my chums' – don't be such a chump.

This is only the beginning. More gentle exercise is needed – get out pounding those country lanes or streets. Breathe in two, three, four, five; hold two, three, four, five; breathe out two, three, four, five. Oh yes, that's more like it.

To test your resolve why not walk past your local pub and gaze through the window to see your friends supping their pints and puffing away? That could well be you standing there, spending money and turning yourself into a zombie for the afternoon. Turn your back on this life, for the next four days at least, and stride out among the hedgerows.

Start to take an interest in the flowers and trees. Spot the shy little celandine hiding away and think of that fine poem by Wordsworth, 'To the Small Celandine'.

> There is a flower, the Lesser Celandine,
> That shrinks like many more from cold and rain,
> And the first moment that the sun may shine,
> Bright as the sun himself, 'tis out again.

How like the Lesser Celandine we are, and now for a delicious lunch.

LUNCH

Borsch

A sort of Russian penicillin posing as a soup.

Serves 4

225 g (8 oz) raw beetroots, plus 1 additional
  beetroot to liquidise into juice
1.25 litres (2¼ pints) good beef or other stock
  – you can use the liquid tubs of stock you
  can now buy in supermarkets or, better still,
  make some home-made
1 teaspoon red wine vinegar or lemon juice, or
  to taste
1 teaspoon sugar
Cayenne pepper
Small quantity of soured cream

Peel the beetroots, chop small and cook them slowly
in the stock for about 1 hour. Strain and add the
vinegar or lemon juice, sugar and a little cayenne
pepper to taste. Add the juice of the extra uncooked
beetroot to heighten the taste and colour of the
borsch. Serve with a dollop of soured cream in each
bowl.

2

Gazpacho

A cold soup from Andalucia, packed with good things, best made with abandon to Bizet's *Carmen*.

Serves 6–8

1.5 kg (3¼ lb) ripe tomatoes, skinned and roughly chopped (choose ones that have a really good flavour)
2 medium green peppers, cored, seeded and chopped into chunks
2 small onions, chopped
2 cucumbers, peeled and chopped
8 tablespoons red wine or sherry vinegar
1 teaspoon chopped fresh tarragon or ¼ teaspoon dried
½ teaspoon sugar
2 cloves of garlic, chopped
250 ml (8 fl oz) tomato juice
250 ml (8 fl oz) iced water
Salt
Ice cubes

For the croûtons
100 g (4 oz) butter
2 slices of white bread, crusts removed, cut into small cubes
2 cloves of garlic, crushed (optional)

For the side dishes:
Cucumber, green pepper, tomatoes, onions, all finely diced

Put all the ingredients except the garnishes into a food processor (in several batches) and whizz until smooth. Taste and season as required before chilling it very well – for at least 3 hours.

To make the croûtons, melt the butter in a heavy frying pan. Add the bread cubes and cook gently, stirring and turning well, until they are golden and crunchy. Drain on kitchen paper and let them cool down. If you like garlic, add the crushed garlic to the pan when you are frying the bread. When you are serving the soup, pass round the garnishes and croûtons in separate little dishes.

Rice with Olives (*Arroz y Aceituna*)

One of the monks' favourite dishes.

Serves 4

3 tablespoons extra virgin olive oil
1 large onion, finely chopped
4 cloves of garlic, finely chopped
350g (12 oz) long-grain rice
1 teaspoon cayenne pepper
1 wineglass dry sherry
600 ml (1 pint) chicken stock (home-made or buy
*   one of the ready-made liquid stocks in tubs)*
A pinch of saffron strands
225 g (8 oz) frozen peas
4 tablespoons chopped parsley
20 black olives, sliced and pitted
Salt and freshly ground black pepper
Lemon juice

Heat the oil in a large frying pan, add the onion and garlic and cook until they are golden – about 5–8 minutes. Then add the rice, stirring well so that all the rice is coated in the lovely oil. Pop in the cayenne pepper and cook for 1 minute, then pour in the sherry. (Take a quick sip first, of course.)

Bring up to the boil and simmer for a minute or so – how long will depend on whether or not you are using an old monastery wood-burning stove on wood mark 6 – until the liquid has reduced by half. Add the chicken stock and saffron. Whack on the lid and cook for around 15 minutes, until the rice has absorbed most of the liquid. Add the peas, parsley, olives, salt and pepper to taste and cook for a further 5 minutes, until all the liquid has been taken up by the rice.

Sprinkle with lemon juice and serve in rough earthenware bowls. It is nourishing and tasty and the monks love it to bits.

Hot Chicken Salad

I first made this for Harold and Madge on the *Neighbours* set in Melbourne. It is refreshing and easy – and full of good things.

Serves 4

4 × 150g (6oz) boneless chicken breasts,
  skinned
2 tablespoons plain flour
4 tablespoons sesame seeds
2 tablespoons olive oil
2 tablespoons fresh shiitake or button
  mushrooms, wiped
4 crunchy spring onions, trimmed and
  chopped
1 clove of garlic, crushed
2.5 cm (1 inch) piece of fresh root ginger, fried
  in deep fat, then chopped
1 teaspoon coriander seeds, crushed
4 tomatoes, skinned and quartered
2 tablespoons balsamic vinegar
Salt and freshly ground black pepper
Variety of lettuce leaves: for example, cos,
  lollo rosso, oak leaf, Chinese leaves, to serve

Cut each chicken breast into 4–6 pieces. Dust with flour and roll in the sesame seeds. Pop into a roasting tin and roast in a preheated oven, 200°C/400°F (gas mark 6), for 15–20 minutes, until tender.

Heat the oil in a large frying pan or wok and tip in the cooked chicken, mushrooms, spring onions, garlic, ginger, coriander seeds and tomatoes. Cook for 2–3 minutes, stirring all the while, then add the vinegar and season to taste with salt and pepper. Stir through and serve immediately on a bed of lettuce leaves.

Grilled Sardines with Tomato, Basil and Onion Salad

The best way to do this is to light your barbecue – it doesn't matter if there is snow on the ground, it is very bracing and the fresh air will do you good. Wait until the flames have died down and the embers have turned a dull pink. Then put six 'plumptious' sardines on to the grill.

Incidentally, my chums in Spain, who buy their sardines fresh from the sea, keep their heads, tails and entrails firmly intact. As the sardines have probably been frozen before I buy them in my local supermarket, I prefer to slit them along the belly and remove the innards. Wash the fish under cold running water and rub the insides with sea salt, removing any black matter in the cavity. Score the sardines with 3 diagonal cuts on each side; brush with a little oil. Grill for about 6–8 minutes, turning once, until they are nice and crispy on the outside and jolly juicy inside. Eat with your hands – it is rather like playing the harmonica really. Serve with a simple salad of sliced tomatoes, finely sliced onion, a sprinkling of coarsely torn fresh basil, with dressing.

Oily fish is quite wonderful for the heart. However, I feel sorely tempted to wash this lot down with a fruity red wine – but I mustn't. Not even a glass?

2

BREAKFAST

Half a melon, a pint of water with the juice of 1 lemon – pure and simple – then yoghurt, fruit and toast. In order to make this rather dull but necessary repast more interesting I play Bill Haley and his Comets singing 'Shake, Rattle and Roll' – the one that starts, 'Get into the kitchen and rattle those pots and pans'. I have my own dance routine worked out as I deseed the melon and squeeze my lemon; it is far too complicated to describe here, but all my friends are most impressed. I especially like Mr Haley's line: 'I'm a one-eyed cat, sitting in a seafood stall', which is wonderfully descriptive. I'm sure vintage rock and roll is about to have another rebirth. I do hope so.

Presumably, you've taken some gentle exercise? Promise me you are not shirking and that you have cycled at least three or four miles after breakfast. Have a good look in the mirror. Notice the clear eye and the healthy glow – you are over halfway.

Tomato and Mozzarella Salad

Serves 4

675 g (1½ lb) lovely plum tomatoes that you can now buy in season from supermarkets
150 g (6 oz) Mozzarella cheese – buffalo Mozzarella is best
1 small sweet red onion, cut thinly into rings
2 tablespoons pine nuts
3 basil leaves, coarsely torn

For the dressing:

6 tablespoons extra virgin olive oil
1 tablespoon balsamic vinegar
2 teaspoons lemon juice
Salt and freshly ground black pepper

Cut the tomatoes into thin slices, around 5 mm (¼ inch) thick and do the same with the Mozzarella. Arrange them in alternate overlapping layers on a large serving dish and as artistically as possible sprinkle the onion rings over them. Scatter over the basil leaves and pine nuts.

A good way to make the dressing is to put all the ingredients into a screwtop jar and give it a good shake. Then drizzle it over the salad and eat immediately.

Runner Beans Fresh from the Garden

What joy!

Half fill a saucepan with water, add a little salt and put on to boil. When the bubbles start to rise nip out into the garden with your favourite bowl and start to pick your runner beans. Make sure they are not too big otherwise they will taste like old gardening gloves. The ideal size is around 7 to 9 inches. Pick away, humming to yourself and perhaps singing a little ditty. When I'm in my garden I usually sing 'Green grow the rushes, O!' – you know the one that ends with 'Three, three the rivals, Two, two the lilywhite boys covered all in green, O! One is one and all alone and ever more shall be so.'

This is not just a fine bean-picking song, it was also sung by the defenders, many of whom were British, at the Battle of the Alamo. Apparently, the words of the song coming from inside this beleaguered fort used to make the attacking Mexicans very cross indeed. They would jump up and down on their sombreros, shake their fists and blow trumpets to try and drown out this ancient ballad. That is why the British and Americans are known to the Mexicans, even to this day, as Gringos – but I digress.

Once you have picked enough beans, say a couple of dozen, run, yes, run, as fast as you can before the sugar in the beans turns to starch, back to your kitchen. Remove any bits of stalk and peel the beans taking off the 'stringy' bits from both sides of the bean. Slice the vegetables into thirds and plonk into the now boiling water for about 5 minutes. The beans should be firm and very slightly crunchy. Serve with a knob of butter and a generous grind of black pepper. Eat with gusto and a fork.

The only trouble with this dish is that when you start singing 'Green grow the rushes, O!', it stays with you the rest of the day and night into the early hours. As you turn over for the umpteenth time your brain is saying for the five hundred and sixtieth time, 'Two, two the lilywhite boys covered all in green, O! One is one and all alone and ever more shall be so.'

Mushrooms on Toast

Use only the whitest, fattest and freshest mushrooms for this. Of course, the best way is to put on your favourite gumboots and trudge through the cow pastures looking for those tell-tale specks of whiteness hiding beneath the dewy grass and spiders' webs as a thin sun begins to warm the day.

Serves 4

225 g (8 oz) mushrooms
25 g (1 oz) butter
1 tablespoon lemon juice
Salt and freshly ground black pepper
1 tablespoon double cream
Chopped parsley
4 triangles of hot buttered toast

Place the mushrooms in a pan with the butter and lemon juice and cook gently for about 5 minutes, until they are tender and the liquid has evaporated. Season with salt and pepper to taste. Stir in the cream and a little parsley.

Spoon on to the hot buttered toast triangles and serve immediately.

3

Now, an afternoon of exercise. You will be so much fitter than on Day 1. You will be able to walk up the hills without stopping, breathing deeply as you go. It is time to reflect seriously upon your life, to take stock of things dear to you. It is possibly the right time to say 'no' for ever to lunchtime drinking.

> **How many times have you been to the pub, not because you really wanted a drink but because you welcomed the company?**

How often have you limited yourself beforehand to one pint and ended up having four? How many afternoons have been written off by this nonsensical activity? As you stride through the country lanes, promise yourself a change of direction. Do things because you want to and not out of boredom or insecurity. Ask yourself, Do I really need a drink, or can I wait till half past five? In no time at all you will be healthier, wealthier and a great deal wiser.

Okay, sermon over.

DINNER, DAY 3

Chicken Couscous

One of the problems with diets of any kind is that the food is not sufficiently cheering – consequently we tend to feel a little downhearted at the prospect of dinner. Well, this is a wonderfully happy dish that will please the eye, bolster the spirits and satisfy the inner man or woman.

Serves 4

1.5 kg (3½ lb) free-range chicken, jointed
3 tablespoons olive oil
2 tablespoons clarified butter, see the
    note * on page 98
1 onion, sliced
1 large ripe tomato
1 cinnamon stick
Salt
½ teaspoon freshly ground black pepper
3 tablespoons chickpeas, soaked overnight and
    drained
3 or 4 baby turnips, quartered
2 courgettes, sliced
225 g (8 oz) precooked couscous
Butter, if you like
Few tablespoons harissa (spicy chilli paste),
    available from delicatessens

Mix together the chicken, oil, butter, onion, tomato, cinnamon, a little salt and the pepper in a large, heavy-based pan. Cook over a medium heat, stirring to coat and brown the chicken. After about 5 minutes, cover with about 350 ml (12 fl oz) cold water and bring to the boil. Pop in the chickpeas, cover and simmer for 30–40 minutes, or until the chicken is tender. Lift out the chicken pieces and put to one side.

3

Continue to cook the mixture in the pan, until the chickpeas are tender – perhaps another 1½ hours – adding the turnips and courgettes about ½ an hour before the end of cooking. Add more water if necessary.

Meanwhile, cover the couscous with water and leave to absorb the liquid for 10–15 minutes. About 15 minutes before the end of the cooking time, put the couscous over the stew to steam (ideally it should be put into a muslin-lined steamer or *cous-cousière*, but a wire sieve lined with a J-cloth will do). Cover with the pan lid to prevent the steam escaping, and steam for 15 minutes. Remove the couscous and keep warm. Pop the chicken back into the pan to heat through and stir a little butter if you wish into the couscous before serving.

Spread the couscous over a warmed serving dish and pile the chicken and vegetables on top with a cupful or so of the liquid. Scatter with the parsley. Spread some of the *harissa* on the chicken and hand the rest round separately.

*To make clarified butter**, melt some unsalted butter over a low heat in a pan, skim off the scum that floats to the top and leave the remainder to rest. You will see a sort of milky mixture floating to the bottom. Carefully pour off or strain the clear liquid from the top, and that is clarified butter.

Sliced Raw Fish (Sashimi)

Only the very freshest of fish should be used for this dish. Forget about frozen fish, look your fishmonger straight in the eye and inquire, 'Was this fish landed this morning?' If there is the slightest hesitation, then forget it.

Serves 4

450g (1 lb) fresh, fresh fish fillets (use sea bass, sea bream, halibut, salmon or tuna), skinned and boned

To serve:
1 carrot } *peeled, pared into thin*
1 white radish (daikon) } *strips and soaked in iced water until needed*
Few tablespoons Japanese soy sauce (shoyu)
Wasabi paste (Japanese green horseradish paste)
Few spring onions, trimmed and finely chopped
Lemon wedges

Wash the fish in plenty of icy-cold water. Pat dry with kitchen paper or a cloth. Slice some of the fish into pieces about 1 cm (¼ inch) thick and 2.5 cm (1 inch) wide, and the rest into paper-thin slices. Arrange simply and attractively on individual serving plates, garnished with the pared carrot and radish. Serve the soy sauce, *wasabi*, spring onions and lemon wedges in separate bowls. The fish is then dipped into the soy sauce and *wasabi* and eaten. Warm plain boiled rice can also be served with it.

3

Moncho's Salmon

This is a delicious dish taught me by my dear chum, Moncho Vilas, a proud Galician restaurateur who first introduced me to the monks of Osera.

Serves 4

4 × 175–225 g (6–8 oz) salmon fillets
50 g (2 oz) seasoned flour
4 tablespoons olive oil
1 large onion, finely chopped
2 cloves of garlic, crushed
675 g (1½ lb) clams in their shells, well
   scrubbed
300 ml (½ pint) fish stock (make your own or
   resort to a tub of the liquid stock you can
   now buy for speed)
1 wineglass dry white wine
3 tablespoons lemon juice
A handful of chopped parsley
1 teaspoon mustard paste
Salt and freshly ground black pepper

Dust the salmon fillets in the seasoned flour and pop them to one side. Heat the oil in a very large frying pan and sauté the onion and garlic for 2–3 minutes, until softened. Lay the salmon in the pan and cook the fillets for 2 minutes on each side.

Add the clams, fish stock, wine, lemon juice and parsley to the pan and cook for about 5 minutes – be careful as the salmon and clams must not overcook.

Just before serving, stir the mustard paste through the sauce and season with a little extra salt and pepper if you need to. Serve with a fresh, green salad and some crusty, wholemeal bread.

4

The usual breakfast – this time accompanied by the strains of Eddie Cochran singing 'Three Steps to Heaven'. Think of your melon as step one. Step two, pour yourself a glass of water and step three, add to it the juice of 1 lemon. Now change the record and put on Little Richard's 'Tutti Frutti'. Create a colourful fruit salad using, say, a pear, peach, mango, apple, pineapple and the remainder of the melon. As you chop them, be careful not to get too carried away, 'Tutti frutti on a rooti' etc. (You might have to play the record a couple of times before the salad is complete; be careful of your fingers.) Finally, add a small pot of creamy yoghurt to the fruit, preferably during the closing bars of the song, 'A wop, bop, a loo bop, wham, bam, boo.' It is quite refreshing and the fruit salad is pretty good too.

And now for a cautionary tale on the evils of drink and how alcohol can alter the future and affect your whole life, concerning my chum Hector – ponder his plight as you exercise those limbs and work up an appetite for lunch.

Hector shouldn't have gone back to Alisdair's house that afternoon. He'd already consumed four or five pints at lunchtime, in the nice pub by the river. Anyway, the point was, he did. Alisdair is, after all, an engaging sort of a chap. An ex-Marine commando captain and the owner of a small distillery in the Scottish lowlands – the perfect credentials for a jolly nice chum.

'Come back, my dear chap, and try the twelve-year-old malt, you'll like it, I know you will.'

I think I've already mentioned that Hector is a doctor, a very good one. His wife Naomi is terribly proud of him and, after weeks of browbeating, she persuaded him to become a representative for the GPs on the Regional Health Committee. After a few months on this it became clear that Hector's star was on the ascent. His natural wit and charm, combined with a strong professional instinct, made him popular. It was not long before his colleagues looked upon him as the next Chairman – a high honour indeed.

Alisdair's Scotch was exceedingly good, peaty and sweet and with just a delicate hint of seaweed because the distillery was near the coast. And Alisdair's stories of life in the Marines were thrilling. Hector had a few hours to spare before his meeting with the Minister for Health, local MPs and various colleagues from the Health Authority. He was planning to go home to change first but

Alisdair's stories, not to mention the whisky, were too good to miss.

Wonderful stories of ambush and subterfuge in the Oman. Alisdair and his platoon would dress up as locals and hide out for weeks at a time in the desert. The vehicles they used looked like chunky beach buggies with very thick tyres and were armed with light machine guns and an assortment of anti-personnel weapons. Alisdair was evidently some sort of hero in the desert, there were photographs of him being carried on the shoulders of some fierce-looking chaps waving their rifles around.

Anyway, the whisky and the stories of derring do made for a jolly sort of *Boys' Own* adventure. Hector could imagine himself watching the sun sink over the Oman desert, a goat roasting away on a spit and his chaps busy cleaning their rifles. His steely eyes would scan the horizon in search of the rebels . . . Gosh, the whisky was very good and it certainly beat listening to people complaining of chest pains and being lethargic all the time.

It was with great reluctance that Hector stepped into the taxi to be taken to the new hotel, one of a chain, for the meeting. He was already half an hour late and was quite surprised to see some of his chums from the Committee, along with the local politicians and an assortment of bigwigs, sitting in a group at the far end of the bar. The room was dimly lit and a pianist was playing an indescribably boring tune on the piano. There were many palms and other plants scattered around the room, the perfect place for an ambush.

No one from the group had seen him arrive and all eyes seemed to be focused on the Chairman, who was sitting with his back to him. No doubt he was saying something frightfully interesting about hospital closures, staff redundancies, zero budgeting . . . all that gobbledegook that grown-up people in suits and shirts with cufflinks talk about.

Needless to say, Hector wasn't terribly keen on closing hospitals or reducing the staffing levels for the health service, but it wouldn't 'do' to make his true feelings known, in these recession-led times.

He was only a few feet away from them now and only one of his colleagues, Chris, spotted him lurking behind a big potted palm. For some strange unaccountable reason Hector thought it would be a brilliant idea to spring like a panther from his hiding place and grab the unsuspecting Chairman in a headlock. It would, he thought, make a wonderful, surprising entrance and then he could apologise to everyone for being late. Yes, said his befuddled brain, a very, very good way to break the ice. It was too late to reconsider. The whisky had done its worst, it wasn't a mild-mannered GP and committee member who hid behind the palm. No! It was Hector of Oman, the scourge of the rebel forces, armed to the teeth with his trusty commando dagger and revolver. (Perhaps I should mention that Hector's favourite film is *Lawrence of Arabia*, but you've probably guessed that already!)

With an alarming bound Hector leapt, as only a sixteen-stone man with nearly a bottle of Scotch on board can leap, and threw his forearm around the throat of the innocent Chairman.

'Ha, ha! You swine,' said Hector in his best Peter O'Toole accent. (Not that Peter O'Toole would ever utter anything so unoriginal.)

All eyes looked at Hector, not with amusement and laughter, but with puzzlement. Hector increased the pressure on the Chairman's thorax and the stool gave way from under him. Now the Chairman's throat, held in Hector's strong grip, was supporting his entire weight. The looks of puzzlement gave way to utter bewilderment and then to panic. Hector was quite astonished that no one was laughing, or even finding it mildly funny. The Minister for Health and his cohorts watched incredulously and it wasn't until someone, probably one of the Minister's minders, grabbed Hector roughly and pushed him unceremoniously aside that the Chairman was eventually rescued.

Everyone avoided Hector from then on and even the Minister was overheard asking pertinent questions on the state of Hector's health.

The next morning Hector woke up from a deep untroubled sleep. He opened his eyes; the bedroom was full of spring sunshine. A glance at the bedside digital alarm told him it was ten to ten. He had slept well. The grating beat of a vacuum cleaner could be heard downstairs. Hector always associated its relentless raucous whine with discomfort and disharmony. He could tell by the rhythm of the vacuum cleaner's sweeps that Naomi was in a bad mood. Long sweeps indicate that all is happy with the world, short erratic ones spell trouble. What could she be upset about?

Then the memories of last night flooded back. Drinking with Alisdair, going to the meeting. Oh my God! How terrible! How utterly, utterly terrible.

It couldn't have been as bad as that, surely? He picked up the phone to call Chris.

'How's the head?' asked Chris.

The panic of realisation had totally overcome the physical discomfort of the hangover. 'Oh fine,' pretended Hector. 'How um, was last night? . . . um . . . I can't remember much about it.'

'Where do you want me to start?' Chris said, obviously embarrassed.

4

'Well, how was I?' inquired Hector in a soft, frightened little voice, the sort of voice Piglet would have used after getting terribly lost in the woods.

'You were . . .'

(Go on, say it, thought Hector, entertaining, amusing, very funny indeed . . . the Minister was most impressed by you. How do you do it, you bastard? You were charming, intelligent and witty etc., etc.)

'You were,' said Chris, pausing as if searching for the correct adjective, 'terrible. In all the years I've known you I have never seen you in such a state.'

Hector's brain went numb, except for registering the odd phrase 'appalling, senseless, disgusting behaviour, everyone was affronted.'

These words were like poison-tipped arrows and every one found its mark.

The beat of the Hoover seemed to synchronise with his pulse. God, she was in a bad mood. Presumably the word had got out.

After Chris had rung off Hector pulled the covers over his head. His life, like a car freewheeling downhill, had hit a sharp bend. The brakes had failed and Hector found himself upside down in the cow pasture of life. The noise of the Hoover was coming closer, it was on the stairs now. Hector pulled the covers tight. Never again would he drink to excess. Never again would he ever attend another committee meeting, listen to all of that excruciating drivel, be pleasant to people he couldn't stand, leave a blazing hearth and a really good film with Helen Mirren in it for a cold draughty committee room . . . presenting long tedious quarterly reports instead of fishing a fast Devon stream in the soft evening light . . . never ever again.

Trout, Hemingway-style

This is a wonderful dish Ernest Hemingway discovered and recorded in his articles on trout fishing. He came across the method in Switzerland and pronounced it: 'the finest way to cook this delicate fish doing full justice to its delicate flavour.'

I can imagine Hemingway sitting on the banks of a swiftly flowing alpine stream with his trusty Primus stove preparing this simple, healthy meal. Passionate conversation would flow with his companions, no doubt centred on love, war, sex and fishing, as the whisky bottle was passed around while the trout simmered away.

If possible, cook this splendid dish in the open air surrounded by wild primroses, violets and bluebells. Eat with gusto soaking up spring's warm sunshine and the pleasing murmur of distant bees.

1 × 175 g (6 oz) trout per person, scaled,
*   cleaned and gutted*
1 wineglass white wine vinegar
2 bay leaves
Couple of dashes of Tabasco sauce or 1
*   teaspoon chilli sauce*

Put the trout in a pan of boiling water that you have seasoned with the vinegar, bay leaves and Tabasco or chilli. Simmer for 4 minutes or so, until the trout turns blue. Serve with lemon wedges, new potatoes and a crisp watercress salad.

By the way, if you are interested in catching your very own trout either get up terribly early or leave it until the early evening. I call these the golden times and they are the periods where the fish feel at their most active and hungry.

Look for a pool away from the main flow of water, preferably overhung with trees and out of the direct sunlight. Keep well away from where you think the fish are and do not clump around on the riverbank or make a sound. Try and use, as an access point, a spot at least twenty yards upstream so that you can drift your bait gaily downstream on the current and, with any luck, it should naturally arrive at your chosen pool. The fish will be lying there in the slow current occasionally snaffling at a passing fly or a grub that has fallen from the overhanging branches.

Unlike my chum Hector, who fishes only with a dry fly, I treat the trout rather like the discerning customers in my restaurant. In my trusty fishing bag I will have an assortment of baits. There will be a few red worms fresh from the compost heap in my garden, some wriggly maggots and a mixture of wet flies – these are feathery things that sink and are supposed to represent a helpless and drowning aphid. I shall take with me a half-a-dozen or so plump pink prawns, boiled with their heads and tails on. Use one for bait and have the rest in a nice sandwich on the riverbank, yum, yum. Also, I shall carry with me some spinners, which are little metal things that look like spoons. However, once they are pulled through the water they transform themselves into shiny, darting fish that the hungry trout will find irresistible.

In some rivers this method of fishing is highly illegal simply because the local angling club, like Hector, believe that the respectable way to catch trout, or any game fish, is with a dry fly. However, I fish the same way I have always done from the first time I picked up a fishing rod when I was seven years old. I believe fish are jolly crafty and sneaky things and that you have to try every trick in the book in order to tempt them into the frying pan. You really have to entice them with the freshest and most delicious of bait. A nice fat worm floating downstream is the equivalent to them of a lobster dinner – impossible to say no to.

Fishing is a brilliant hobby and is well suited to this detoxification plan as it provides fresh air, gentle exercise and, with any luck, lunch on the riverbank. But if you are unsuccessful by, say, eleven o'clock in the morning, nip round to your friendly local trout farm. Once there pay the man a couple of quid, cast your worm into the nearest pond and I'll guarantee lunch is only seconds away.

Trout in Newspaper

This is another wonderful way to cook trout. Remember to use only the serious newspapers. I find the trout cooks beautifully in *The Independent*.

1 × 175 g (6 oz) trout per person, scaled,
*   cleaned and gutted*
2 sheets of newspaper per person
1 tablespoon mixed chopped herbs – for
*   example, fennel leaves, parsley, thyme and*
*   chervil – per fish*
1 wedge of lemon per fish
Knob of butter per fish
Freshly ground black pepper

Stuff the fish with the herbs and lemon. Wrap the paper round each fish to form a parcel and run under the cold water tap until sodden.

Pop into a preheated oven, 180°C/350°F (gas mark 4), for about 8 minutes, until the paper dries out completely. With a pair of scissors open the package and peel off the paper, which will lift off the skin of the trout. Serve with the lemon and butter and mill over plenty of pepper. New potatoes and a green salad make a good accompaniment.

Greek Country Salad

To make this a more substantial supper, I eat this with a couple of thick slices of crusty bread.

Serves 4

1 crisp lettuce
½ cucumber
4 firm ripe tomatoes
1 large sweet onion, thinly sliced in rings
225 g (8 oz) Feta cheese, crumbled
About a dozen or more black olives
1 bunch of flat-leaf parsley or mint, coarsely
    chopped

For the dressing:

4 tablespoons olive oil
Juice of ½ lemon
pinch of sugar
Salt and freshly ground black pepper

Separate the lettuce leaves and use to line a salad bowl. Cut the cucumber into quarters lengthways, reassemble and slice. Cut the tomatoes into wedges.

To make the dressing, mix together the oil, lemon juice, sugar and salt and pepper. Toss all the other ingredients in the dressing, pile into the middle of the lettuce, and serve.

Hake or Bream in a Salt Crust

This dish tastes as if it has been cooked in the sea.

Serves 4

100g (4oz) softened butter
1 teaspoon chopped tarragon
A small handful of chopped parsley
3 cloves of garlic, chopped
Salt and freshly ground black pepper
1 × 1.25 kg (3 lb) hake, bream or bass, scaled,
  gutted and washed
2.75 kg (6 lb) coarse sea salt
Melted butter and wedges of lemon, to serve

Mix together the butter, tarragon, parsley, garlic, salt and pepper, adding the roe too if the fish has it. Stuff all this into the belly of the fish and sew up the opening.

Put a layer of salt in a big, deep casserole up to a depth of 3 cm (1½ inches) and pop the fish on its back on top. Cover completely with the rest of the salt. Bake in a preheated oven, 220°C/425°F (gas mark 7), for about 35 minutes.

Take care as you remove the casserole from your oven, as it will be very hot. Knock the bottom of the casserole if you need to, to loosen the salt block. Then carefully knock the salt from around the fish. Serve at once with the hot melted butter and lemon wedges, accompanied by a green salad.

Retire early unless there is a good play on the television with Helen Mirren in it. Tomorrow is your final day.

THE FINAL DAY

*I will arise and go now, and
    go to Innisfree,
And a small cabin build
    there, of clay and wattles
    made:
Nine bean-rows will I have
    there, a hive for the honey
    bee,
And live alone in the bee-loud
    glade.*

W.B. Yeats was walking down the Strand
one day. He was feeling a bit gloomy, a little
depressed actually, when he spotted in a
shop window one of those curious machines
that used to dispense a brand of orange
juice. Part of the advertisement selling the
juice depicted an island and the great poet's
mind was instantly transported to the place
of his dreams. There on the pavement with
motor buses and taxis chugging past, Yeats
started to compose one of the finest poems
that celebrates the joys of nature and salutes
the human spirit, 'The Lake Isle of
Innisfree'.

And, by now, this poem should reflect
your own state of mind and feeling of
optimism. The song of the birds will be
clearer, the scent of the flowers will be
stronger and you will be filled with a new
spark of energy and zest.

So endeth the first lesson.

BREAKFAST

Hooray!

First of all, pour your pint glass of water and line up your melon and lemon neatly on the kitchen table, okay?

Then select Elvis's 'Blue Suede Shoes' and put it on the record player.

One for the money [cut your melon in half]
Two for the show [cut your lemon in half]
Three to get ready [scoop pips from melon]
Now, go cat go [squeeze lemon into a pint glass of water while gyrating like mad].

This is good fun and provides endless seconds of entertainment for all the family. My cat finds it highly amusing. Have some toast or cereal with milk after this burst of activity.

As this is your final day of the detoxification plan go for one last cycle ride. As you ride along try to picture in your mind what it was like to have a dreadful hangover. Remember that awful feeling of nausea, that heavy, muggy head. Recall what it was like to feel anxious and disoriented. Paint a mental picture of yourself feeling cowed and subdued and lacking life's vital spark. Make a little pact with yourself to try very, very hard to avoid such wretched feelings in the future.

Lemon Potatoes

I discovered this quite by chance in a little roadside café in the foothills of the Pyrenees. It is a wonderfully flavoursome way to enjoy the humble spud.

Serves 4

675 g (1½ lb) potatoes
2 tablespoons virgin olive oil
10 cloves of garlic, roughly chopped
Finely grated zest and juice of 1 lemon
4 tablespoons water
6 bay leaves
1 teaspoon thyme
½ teaspoon dried oregano
4 rosemary sprigs
½ teaspoon sugar
Salt and freshly ground black pepper
A bunch of parsley, coarsely chopped

Cut the potatoes into generous bite-sized bits and put them into a casserole dish. Add the olive oil, garlic, lemon zest and juice, water, bay leaves, thyme, oregano, half the rosemary, sugar, salt and pepper -- in fact, all the ingredients apart from the parsley – and give them a good stir round.

Cook the potatoes in a preheated oven, 200°C/400°F (gas mark 6), for about 30–40 minutes, until they are crispy, occasionally stirring and giving them a coating of this lovely flavoured oil. When they are ready garnish with the parsley and the rest of the rosemary.

Fresh Broad Beans and Ham

This is the only recipe in the plan that involves meat, but then beans and ham are a marriage made in heaven.

Serves 4

1.4 kg (3 lb) fresh broad beans
Couple of tablespoons olive oil
1 clove of garlic, chopped
75–100 g (3–4 oz) serrano or prosciutto *ham,*
  or back bacon, chopped
Freshly ground black pepper
Bowl of freshly grated cheese

Shell the beans, keeping the young and tender pods intact, but stringing both sides. Blanch them for 3 minutes in boiling salted water.

Meanwhile, heat your largest frying pan and add the oil, garlic, ham or bacon and the drained beans. Grind over plenty of black pepper and sauté gently until the bacon is cooked and the beans are tender. Serve with the grated cheese.

A Pasta Called Basil

A quick and tasty dish.

Serves 4

900 g (2 lb) fresh spaghetti, fettuccine or
  tagliatelle
1 large handful of basil, chopped
150 ml (¼ pint) extra virgin olive oil
Freshly ground black pepper
Parmesan cheese, finely grated

Cook the pasta in plenty of boiling salted water, until it is just tender but still firm, *al dente*. Drain at once.

Meanwhile, mix the basil and oil in a large bowl.

Add the pasta and toss thoroughly with lots of black pepper. Sprinkle with Parmesan cheese and serve at once with a green salad.

Use the rest of the afternoon to reflect on the things you've discovered in the past five days – go to your favourite place (not the pub) and ponder this new-found wisdom.

And now for some practical advice: if you must drink, and most of us get caught up in the social activity that surrounds alcohol – enjoy it with a trusted chum or, better still, your spouse. For instance, if you have to go to an important function where the fickle finger of fate often dictates your promotion prospects, take precautions. Instruct your chum or spouse to come up with a secret codeword. So when they see you acting a bit strangely and recognise that within a few seconds you will probably make a total idiot of yourself, they can utter the secret watchword. 'Hippopotamus' is quite a good word as it does not normally crop up in everyday conversation. It stands out prominently like the very beast itself.

When your chum or spouse overhears you saying to the chairman's wife, 'I think you have particularly nice breasts, they look wonderfully firm for a woman of your age,' it's time for 'Hippopotamus' to come to the rescue. Your chum should cough and say the magic word, carefully disguised in a sentence so that it will go unnoticed by everyone but you. 'Gosh, I'm so hungry I could eat a hippopotamus', is quite a good one. Or 'the next-door neighbours are thinking of getting a hippopotamus'; this might raise a few eyebrows, though, and may invite unwelcome scrutiny.

Like Cinderella when the clock strikes twelve, you must quickly say your goodnights and leave immediately. Do not dally. You will leave the party with people saying nice things about you and there will not be one sliver of remorse in the morning.

Actually, I think that advice alone is worth the price of this book. So many careers have been broken by crazy utterances in the wee small hours – you have been warned! And now for the last supper.

> *This day is called the feast of Crispian:*
> *He that outlives this day and comes safe home,*
> *Will stand a tip-toe when this day is nam'd,*
> *And rouse him at the name of Crispian.*

That's probably a little over the top as an introduction to a meal but it is all I could find for a stirring finale, from Shakespeare's *Henry V* of course, quoted in my bumper book of boys' poetry.

I have a feeling, gentle reader, that you will feel sorely tempted to go to the pub tonight – and I can't blame you. If you have stuck faithfully to my plan, then you deserve a break and this meal, the last meal in the plan (sniffs onion and wipes away tears), is designed to provide a healthy living for your, now happy, tummy.

5

Salade Niçoise

Serves 4–6

*Hearts of a couple of real lettuces: crisp green
    leaves that are curled tightly together
    (icebergs are good)*
*A handful of lightly cooked runner, French or
    broad beans*
8 ripe tomatoes, sliced
2 green tomatoes, sliced
½ teaspoon salt
5–6 tablespoons virgin olive oil
8 free-range, hard-boiled eggs, halved
*100 g (4 oz) black olives that have been
    marinated in oil*
275 g (9 oz) tinned tuna fish in olive oil, flaked
*100 g (4 oz) tinned anchovy fillets in olive oil,
    cut into pieces*
1 small tin sardines in olive oil, cut into pieces

Wash and thoroughly dry the lettuce and put into a
large salad bowl. Add the beans, tomatoes, salt and
olive oil. Using your fingers, carefully turn the salad
until everything is coated with oil and salt.

Add all the remaining ingredients and, still using
your fingers, gently mix them together. Bring the eggs
and olives to the top, then serve.

Garlic Chicken (*Pollo Adobado*)

At the Monastery of Osera the aroma of this roasting chicken and garlic wafts through the bean rows and melon plots, over the sweet peas and fills the sunny walled garden with the prospect of dinner.

8 free-range chicken drumsticks

For the marinade you need:

4 tablespoons extra virgin olive oil
6 cloves of garlic, roughly chopped
½ onion, finely chopped
Juice of 1 lemon, plus 2 teaspoons finely grated
*   zest*
2 teaspoons cayenne pepper
2 teaspoons paprika
1 teaspoon cumin seeds
3 whole cloves
Pinch of saffron strands
3 tablespoons dry sherry
1 tablespoon sugar

Put all the marinade ingredients into a bowl (not aluminium) and stir well.

Slash each drumstick three or four times with a sharp knife and pop into the bowl, stirring to ensure that each piece of chicken is covered with the marinade. Leave for 30 minutes at least.

Lift out the chicken and put in a roasting dish. Pour on generous spoonfuls of the oily marinade and make sure that the chicken drumsticks are speckled with the little chunks of garlic. Roast in a preheated oven, 200°C/400°F (gas mark 6), until crisp and tender – about 40 minutes.

Eat with a green salad made with crispy cos or Little Gem lettuce and baby spinach leaves and chunks of freshly baked wholemeal bread.

Yum, yum.

EPILOGUE

So there you have it. The Floyd-Pritchard guide to a healthier way of life. We have just completed the plan and are raring to go again. In fact, we are feeling so good that we have just spent the morning playing with David's frisbee. And because our bodies are cleansed, our livers have been rinsed and refreshed, our eyes are sparkling and there is a spring in our steps, we might celebrate with just a couple of small glasses of dry white wine before we hop on to a plane and whizz off to the Far East for another three months of filming, erratic meals, mayhem and madness.

But no one will have to drag us to the plane. We are fit, we are happy, we are relaxed and though we have walked through the valley of the shadow of death – or whatever that psalm goes on about – we have that virtuous, smug, self-righteous feeling that only the reformed can.

As Tom Waite said on his album *Bounced Cheques* (that reminds me of something I must attend to immediately), 'The piano has been drinking, not me. Not me.'

Good health, good luck, God bless, goodbye and best dishes, with love.

Index

Recipes are printed in bold type